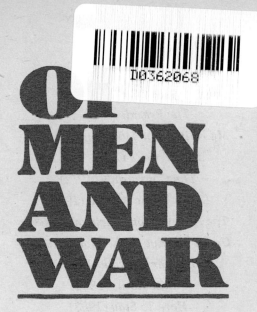

OF MEN AND WAR

Also by JOHN HERSEY

Blues (1987)

The Call (1985)

The Walnut Door (1977)

The President (1975)

My Petition for More Space (1974)

The Writer's Craft (1974)

The Conspiracy (1972)

Letter to the Alumni (1970)

The Algiers Motel Incident (1968)

Under the Eye of the Storm (1967)

Too Far To Walk (1966)

White Lotus (1965)

Here To Stay (1963)

The Child Buyer (1960)

The War Lover (1959)

A Single Pebble (1956)

The Marmot Drive (1953)

The Wall (1950)

Hiroshima (1946)

A Bell for Adano (1944)*

Into the Valley (1943)

*Winner of the 1945 Pulitzer Prize

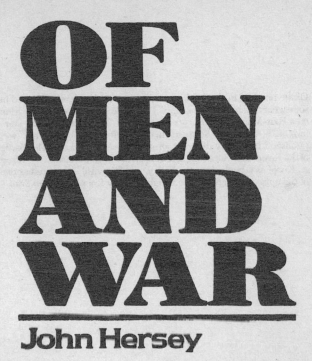

OF MEN AND WAR

John Hersey

If you purchased this book without a cover, you should be aware that this book is stolen property. It was reported as "unsold and destroyed" to the publisher, and neither the author nor the publisher has received any payment for this "stripped book."

SCHOLASTIC INC.
New York Toronto London Auckland Sydney

Of the material in this book, the following articles were published in somewhat different form in *Life:* "The Battle of the River," "Nine Men on a Four-Man Raft," "*Borie's* Last Battle," "Front Seats at Sea War" (originally titled "P.T. Squadron in the South Pacific"). "Survival" was published in slightly different form in *The New Yorker.* "The Battle of the River" in a more complete version has been published by Alfred A. Knopf as a book, *Into the Valley,* and "Survival" appeared as one of the episodes in another book published by Knopf, *Here To Stay.*

ISBN 0-590-44649-5

12 11 10 9 8 7 6 5 4 3 2 1   9   1 2 3 4 5 6/9

ABOUT THE AUTHOR

John Hersey was born in Tientsin, China,
in 1914 and lived there until 1924, when
his family returned to the United States.
He attended Hotchkiss School, was grad-
uated from Yale in 1936, and then went
to England to study at Clare College,
Cambridge, for one year. Upon his return to this country, he was private
secretary to Sinclair Lewis for a summer.
Hersey has been a writer, editor, and war
correspondent for *Time* and *Life*, a writer
for *The New Yorker* and other magazines.
Since 1947 he has been devoting most of
his time to fiction.

CONTENTS

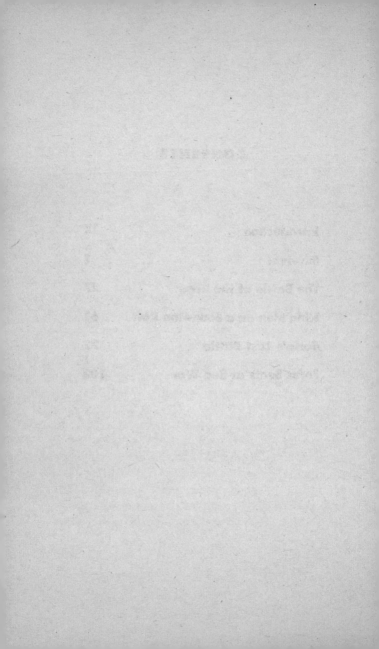

INTRODUCTION

The stories in this book describe some of the sensations of what has come to be called "conventional warfare." This refers to all those forms of war that do not involve the use of atomic weapons.

In another book, *Hiroshima*, I have given an account of what happens to those on whom atomic warfare is waged. Nearly everyone agrees that the most urgent strivings of the world's statesmen must be toward the goal of prohibiting atomic warfare forever—for in it, if it occurs, there will be no victory for anyone, only general disaster for all mankind.

There are some who feel that "conventional" wars not only will be fought in future but even can be justified. I am not one of them. The stories in this volume may help readers to see why warfare, "conventional" or otherwise, cannot be justified as a means of settling disputes between nations, for these are stories of what common men, not neces-

sarily leaders or heroes, feel as they wage war—
and their feelings are inevitably reduced, in the
end, to what men cannot help feeling about their
worst crime, which is murder.

The terrain, the weapons, and the races of war
vary, but certainly never the sensations, except in
degree, for they are as universal as those of love.

On the surface the sensations of war, as these
stories reveal them, may not all *seem* to be sensations of suffering, pain, discomfort, and guilt. Some
seem to be wildly pleasant sensations. I will point
to only one example: the strange, giddy elation of
the men on the bridge of the *U.S.S. Borie* when
they have their adversary, a German submarine,
pinned beneath their ship in a kind of death grip.
But I would suggest that this is a glee of briefest
duration, for it combines two guilty elements: relief
at the thought that the other human being, not the
self, is to die; and, far worse, an upsurging drive
to destroy. This drive is present to some degree in
all of us, but living in a world at peace most of
us succeed in diverting it into acceptable and harm-
less outlets. One of the worst things about war is
that it renders this destructive urge respectable and
even, it appears, praiseworthy. Men have been
known to get medals for displaying it.

It is true that warfare does also provide men
with occasions for selfless generosity toward their
fellows, of a sort that we call heroic sacrifice. The

concern of young Lieutenant John F. Kennedy for his wrecked crewmen, in the now-famous episode of the survival of the youth destined to be President of the United States, and the gentle but costly care of Jim Hosegood for his delirious friend, in the story of the aviators crowded on a too-small rubber raft at sea—these are examples of human love at work under harrowing circumstances. But occasional sacrifice does not justify widespread pain; a hundred heroes do not restore one life unjustly lost.

War does ask courage of men, but so does peace. Indeed, I hope that this book—showing instances of courage and cowardice, of heroism and utter selfishness, of love of life and disgusting bloodlust —will help readers to make a leap of imagination, to arrive at this fact of our time: peace is a far sterner challenge than war. War is the easy way out, the primitive resort to rage and killing. Peace, whether national or personal—the solution of problems without recourse to fighting, yet without compromising principles—requires of us greater stamina, greater sacrifice, greater forbearance, greater endurance, greater patience, greater resourcefulness, greater love, and even greater physical courage, by far, than giving vent to violence.

SURVIVAL

This is the story of a crucial episode in the life of
John F. Kennedy, who, seventeen years after these
events, became President of the United States.

The time of these occurrences was August, 1943.
I wrote the account a few months later, when Kennedy had been returned to the United States for re-
cuperation and for separation, in due course, from
the service. He told me the story one afternoon when
I visited him in the New England Baptist Hospital,
in Boston, where the disc between his fifth lumbar
vertebra and his sacrum, ruptured in his crash in
the Solomons, had been operated upon; and I asked
if I might write it down. He asked me if I wouldn't
talk first with some of his crew, so I went to the
Motor Torpedo Boat Training Centre at Melville,
Rhode Island, and there, under the curving iron of
a Quonset Hut, three enlisted men named Johnston,
McMahon, and McGuire filled in the gaps.

1

It seems that Kennedy's PT, the 109, was out one night with a squadron patrolling Blackett Strait, in mid-Solomons. Blackett Strait is a patch of water bounded on the northeast by the volcano called Kolombangara, on the west by the island of Vella Lavella, on the south by the island of Gizo and a string of coral-fringed islets, and on the east by the bulk of New Georgia. The boats were working about forty miles away from their base on the island of Rendova, on the south side of New Georgia. They had entered Blackett Strait, as was their habit, through Ferguson Passage, between the coral islets and New Georgia.

The night was a starless black and Japanese destroyers were around. It was about two-thirty. The 109, with three officers and ten enlisted men aboard, was leading three boats on a sweep for a target. An officer named George Ross was up on the bow, magnifying the void with binoculars. Kennedy was at the wheel and he saw Ross turn and point into the darkness. The man in the forward machine-gun turret shouted, "Ship at two o'clock!" Kennedy saw a shape and spun the wheel to turn for an attack, but the 109 answered sluggishly. She was running slowly on only one of her three engines, so as to make a minimum wake and avoid detection from the air. The shape became a Japanese destroyer, cutting

3

through the night at forty knots and heading straight for the 109. The thirteen men on the PT hardly had time to brace themselves. Those who saw the Japanese ship coming were paralyzed by fear in a curious way: they could move their hands but not their feet. Kennedy whirled the wheel to the left, but again the 109 did not respond. Ross went through the gallant but futile motions of slamming a shell into the breach of the 37-millimetre anti-tank gun which had been temporarily mounted that very day, wheels and all, on the foredeck. The urge to bolt and dive over the side was terribly strong, but still no one was able to move; all hands froze to their battle stations. Then the Japanese crashed into the 109 and cut her right in two. The sharp enemy forefoot struck the PT on the starboard side about fifteen feet from the bow and crunched diagonally across with a racking noise. The PT's wooden hull hardly even delayed the destroyer. Kennedy was thrown hard to the left in the cockpit, and he thought, "This is how it feels to be killed." In a moment he found himself on his back on the deck, looking up at the destroyer as it passed through his boat. There was another loud noise and a huge flash of yellow-red light, and the destroyer glowed. Its peculiar, raked inverted-Y stack stood out in the brilliant light and, later, in Kennedy's memory.

There was only one man below decks at the moment of collision. That was McMahon, engineer. He had no idea what was up. He was just reaching forward to wrench the starboard engine into gear when a ship came into his engine room. He was lifted from the narrow passage between two of the engines and thrown painfully against the starboard bulkhead aft of the boat's auxiliary generator. He landed in a sitting position. A tremendous burst of flame came back at him from the day room, where some of the gas tanks were. He put his hands over his face, drew his legs up tight, and waited to die. But he felt water hit him after the fire, and he was sucked far downward as his half of the PT sank. He began to struggle upward through the water. He had held his breath since the impact, so his lungs were tight and they hurt. He looked up through the water. Over his head he saw a yellow glow—gasoline burning on the water. He broke the surface and was in fire again. He splashed hard to keep a little island of water around him.

Johnston, another engineer, had been asleep on deck when the collision came. It lifted him and dropped him overboard. He saw the flame and the destroyer for a moment. Then a huge propeller pounded by near him and the awful turbulence of the destroyer's wake took him down, turned him

5

over and over, held him down, shook him, and drubbed on his ribs. He hung on and came up in water that was like a river rapids. The next day his body turned black and blue from the beating.

Kennedy's half of the PT stayed afloat. The bulkheads were sealed, so the undamaged watertight compartments up forward kept the half hull floating. The destroyer rushed off into the dark. There was an awful quiet: only the sound of gasoline burning.

Kennedy shouted, "Who's aboard?"

Feeble answers came from three of the enlisted men, McGuire, Mauer, and Albert; and from one of the officers, Thom.

Kennedy saw the fire only ten feet from the boat. He thought it might reach her and explode the remaining gas tanks, so he shouted, "Over the side!"

The five men slid into the water. But the wake of the destroyer swept the fire away from the PT, so after a few minutes Kennedy and the others crawled back aboard. Kennedy shouted for survivors in the water. One by one they answered: Ross, the third officer; Harris, McMahon, Johnston, Zinsser, Starkey, enlisted men. Two did not answer: Kirksey and Marney, enlisted men. Since the last bombing at base, Kirksey had been sure he would die. He had huddled at his battle station by the fantail gun, with his kapok life jacket tied tight up to his cheeks. No one knows what happened to him or to Marney.

Harris shouted from the darkness, "Mr. Kennedy! Mr. Kennedy! McMahon is badly hurt." Kennedy took his shoes, his shirt, and his sidearms off, told Mauer to blink a light so that the men in the water would know where the half hull was, then dived in and swam toward the voice. The survivors were widely scattered. McMahon and Harris were a hundred yards away.

When Kennedy reached McMahon, he asked, "How are you, Mac?"

McMahon said, "I'm all right. I'm kind of burnt."

Kennedy shouted out, "How are the others?"

Harris said softly, "I hurt my leg."

Kennedy, who had been on the Harvard swimming team five years before, took McMahon in tow and headed for the PT. A gentle breeze kept blowing the boat away from the swimmers. It took forty-five minutes to make what had been an easy hundred yards. On the way in, Harris said, "I can't go any farther." Kennedy, of the Boston Kennedy's, said to Harris, of the same home town, "For a guy from Boston, you're certainly putting up a great exhibition out here, Harris." Harris made it all right and didn't complain any more. Then Kennedy swam

7

from man to man, to see how they were doing. All who had survived the crash were able to stay afloat, since they were wearing life preservers—kapok jackets shaped like overstuffed vests, aviators' yellow Mae Wests, or air-filled belts like small inner tubes. But those who couldn't swim had to be towed back to the wreckage by those who could. One of the men screamed for help. When Ross reached him, he found that the screaming man had two life jackets on. Johnston was treading water in a film of gasoline which did not catch fire. The fumes filled his lungs and he fainted. Thom towed him in. The others got in under their own power. It was now after 5:00 A.M., but still dark. It had taken nearly three hours to get everyone aboard.

The men stretched out on the tilted deck of the PT. Johnston, McMahon, and Ross collapsed into sleep. The men talked about how wonderful it was to be alive and speculated on when the other PT's would come back to rescue them. Mauer kept blinking the light to point their way. But the other boats had no idea of coming back. They had seen a collision, a sheet of flame, and a slow burning on the water. When the skipper of one of the boats saw the sight, he put his hands over his face and sobbed, "My God! My God!" He and the others turned away. Back at the base, after a couple of days, the squadron held services for the souls of the thirteen men, and one of the officers wrote his mother, "George Ross lost his life for a cause that he believed in stronger than any one of us, because he was an idealist in the purest sense. Jack Kennedy, the Ambassador's son, was on the same boat and also lost his life. The man that said the cream of a nation is lost in war can never be accused of making an overstatement of a very cruel fact. . . ."

When day broke, the men on the remains of the 109 stirred and looked around. To the northeast, three miles off, they saw the monumental cone of Kolombangara; there, the men knew, ten thousand Japanese swarmed. To the west, five miles away, they saw Vella Lavella; more Japs. To the south, only a mile or so away, they actually could see a Japanese camp on Gizo. Kennedy ordered his men to keep as low as possible, so that no moving silhouettes would show against the sky. The listing hulk was gurgling and gradually settling. Kennedy said, "What do you want to do if the Japs come out? Fight or surrender?" One said, "Fight with what?" So they took an inventory of their armament. The 37-millimetre gun had flopped over the side and was hanging there by a chain. They had one tommy gun, six 45-calibre automatics, and one .38. Not much.

"Well," Kennedy said, "what do you want to do?"

One said, "Anything you say, Mr. Kennedy. You're the boss."

Kennedy said, "There's nothing in the book about a situation like this. Seems to me we're not a military organization any more. Let's just talk this over."

They talked it over, and pretty soon they argued, and Kennedy could see that they would never survive in anarchy. So he took command again.

It was vital that McMahon and Johnston should have room to lie down. McMahon's face, neck, hands, wrists, and feet were horribly burned. Johnston was pale and he coughed continually. There was scarcely space for everyone, so Kennedy ordered the other men into the water to make room, and went in himself. All morning they clung to the hulk and talked about how incredible it was that no one had come to rescue them. All morning they watched for the plane which they thought would be looking for them. They cursed war in general and PT's in particular. At about ten o'clock the hulk heaved a moist sigh and turned turtle. McMahon and Johnston had to hang on as best they could. It was clear that the remains of the 109 would soon sink. When the sun had passed the meridian, Kennedy said, "We will swim to that small island," pointing to one of a group three miles to the southeast. "We have less chance of making it than some of these other islands here, but there'll be less chance of Japs, too." Those who could not swim well grouped themselves around a long two-by-six timber with which carpenters had braced the 37-millimetre cannon on deck and which had been knocked overboard by the force of the collision. They tied several pairs of shoes to the timber, as well as the ship's lantern, wrapped in a life jacket to keep it afloat. Thom took charge of this unwieldy group. Kennedy took McMahon in tow again. He cut loose one end of a long strap on McMahon's Mae West and took the end in his teeth. He swam breast stroke, pulling the helpless McMahon along on his back. It took over five hours to reach the island. Water lapped into Kennedy's mouth through his clenched teeth, and he swallowed a lot. The salt water cut into McMahon's awful burns, but he did not complain. Every few minutes, when Kennedy stopped to rest, taking the strap out of his mouth and holding it in his hand, McMahon would simply say, "How far do we have to go?"

Kennedy would reply, "We're going good." Then he would ask, "How do you feel, Mac?"

McMahon always answered, "I'm O.K., Mr. Kennedy. How about you?"

In spite of his burden, Kennedy beat the other

11

men to the reef that surrounded the island. He left McMahon on the reef and told him to keep low, so as not to be spotted by Japs. Kennedy went ahead and explored the island. It was only a hundred yards in diameter; coconuts on the trees but none on the ground; no visible Japs. Just as the others reached the island, one of them spotted a Japanese barge chugging along close to shore. They all lay low. The barge went on. Johnston, who was very pale and weak and who was still coughing a lot, said, "They wouldn't come here. What'd they be walking around here for? It's too small." Kennedy lay in some bushes, exhausted by his effort, his stomach heavy with the water he had swallowed. He had been in the sea, except for short intervals on the hulk, for fifteen and a half hours. Now he started thinking. Every night for several nights the PT's had cut through Ferguson Passage on their way to action. Ferguson Passage was just beyond the next little island. Maybe . . .

He stood up. He took one of the pairs of shoes. He put one of the rubber life belts around his waist. He hung the .38 around his neck on a lanyard. He took his pants off. He picked up the ship's lantern, a heavy battery affair ten inches by ten inches, still wrapped in the kapok jacket. He said, "If I find a boat, I'll flash the lantern twice. The password will be 'Roger,' the answer will be 'Willco.'" He walked toward the water. After fifteen paces he was dizzy, but in the water he felt all right.

It was early evening. It took half an hour to swim to the reef around the next island. Just as he planted his feet on the reef, which lay about four feet under the surface, he saw the shape of a very big fish in the clear water. He flashed the light at it and splashed hard. The fish went away. Kennedy remembered what one of his men had said a few days before, "These barracuda will come up under a swimming man and eat his testicles." He had many occasions to think of that remark in the next few hours.

Now it was dark. Kennedy blundered along the uneven reef in water up to his waist. Sometimes he would reach forward with his leg and cut one of his shins or ankles on sharp coral. Other times he would step forward onto emptiness. He made his way like a slow-motion drunk, hugging the lantern. At about nine o'clock he came to the end of the reef, alongside Ferguson Passage. He took his shoes off and tied them to the life jacket, then struck out into open water. He swam about an hour, until he felt he was far enough out to intercept the PT's. Treading water, he listened for the muffled roar of motors, getting chilled, waiting, holding the lamp. Once he looked west and saw flares and the false gaiety of an action. The lights were far beyond the little islands, even beyond Gizo, ten miles away. Kennedy realized that the PT boats had chosen, for the first night in many, to go around Gizo instead of through Ferguson Passage. There was no hope. He started back. He made the same painful promenade of the reef and struck out for the tiny island where his friends were. But this swim was different. He was very tired and now the current was running fast, carrying him to the right. He saw that he could not make the island, so he flashed the light once and shouted "Roger! Roger!" to identify himself.

On the beach the men were hopefully vigilant. They saw the light and heard the shouts. They were very happy, because they thought that Kennedy had found a PT. They walked out onto the reef, sometimes up to their waists in water, and waited. It was very painful for those who had no shoes. The men shouted, but not much, because they were afraid of Japanese.

One said, "There's another flash."

A few minutes later a second said, "There's a light over there."

A third said, "We're seeing things in this dark."

They waited a long time, but they saw nothing except phosphorescence and heard nothing but the sound of waves. They went back, very discouraged.

One said despairingly, "We're going to die."

Johnston said, "Aw, shut up. You can't die. Only the good die young."

Kennedy had drifted right by the little island. He thought he had never known such deep trouble, but something he did shows that unconsciously he had not given up hope. He dropped his shoes, but he held onto the heavy lantern, his symbol of contact with his fellows. He stopped trying to swim. He seemed to stop caring. His body drifted through the wet hours, and he was very cold. His mind was a jumble. A few hours before he had wanted desperately to get to the base at Rendova. Now he only wanted to get back to the little island he had left that night, but he didn't try to get there; he just wanted to. His mind seemed to float away from his body. Darkness and time took the place of a mind in his skull. For a long time he slept, or was crazy, or floated in a chill trance.

The currents of the Solomon Islands are queer. The tide shoves and sucks through the islands and makes the currents curl in odd patterns. It was a fateful pattern into which Jack Kennedy drifted. He drifted in it all night. His mind was blank, but his fist was tightly clenched on the kapok around the lantern. The current moved in a huge circle—west past Gizo, then north and east past Kolombangara, then south into Ferguson Passage. Early in the morning the sky turned from black to gray, and so did Kennedy's mind. Light came to both at about six. Kennedy looked around and saw that he was exactly where he had been the night before when he saw the flares beyond Gizo. For a second time, he started home. He thought for a while that he had lost his mind and that he only imagined that he was repeating his attempt to reach the island. But the chill of the water was real enough, the lantern was real, his progress was measurable. He made the reef, crossed the lagoon, and got to the first island. He lay on the beach awhile. He found that his lantern did not work any more, so he left it and started back to the next island, where his men were. This time the trip along the reef was awful. He had discarded his shoes, and every step on the coral was painful. This time the swim across the gap where the current had caught him the night before seemed endless. But the current had changed; he made the island. He crawled up on the beach. He was vomiting when his men came up to him. He said, "Ross, you try it tonight." Then he passed out.

Ross, seeing Kennedy so sick, did not look forward to the execution of the order. He distracted himself by complaining about his hunger. There were a few coconuts on the trees, but the men were too weak to climb up for them. One of the men thought of sea food, stirred his tired body, and found a snail on the beach. He said, "If we were desperate, we could eat these." Ross said, "Desperate, hell. Give me that. I'll eat that." He took it in his hand and looked at it. The snail put its head out and looked at him. Ross was startled, but he shelled the snail and ate it, making faces because it was bitter.

In the afternoon, Ross swam across to the next island. He took a pistol to signal with, and he spent the night watching Ferguson Passage from the reef around the island. Nothing came through. Kennedy slept badly that night; he was cold and sick.

The next morning everyone felt wretched. Planes which the men were unable to identify flew overhead and there were dogfights. That meant Japs as well as friends, so the men dragged themselves into the bushes and lay low. Some prayed. Johnston said, "You guys make me sore. You didn't spend ten cents in church in ten years, then all of a sudden you're in trouble and you see the light." Kennedy felt a little better now. When Ross came back, Kennedy decided that the group should move to another, larger island to the southeast, where there seemed to be more coconut trees and where the party would be nearer Ferguson Passage. Again Kennedy took McMahon in tow with the strap in his teeth, and the nine others grouped themselves around the timber.

This swim took three hours. The nine around the timber were caught by the current and barely made the far tip of the island. Kennedy found walking the quarter mile across to them much harder than the three-hour swim. The cuts on his bare feet were festered and looked like small balloons. The men were suffering most from thirst, and they broke open some coconuts lying on the ground and avidly drank the milk. Kennedy and McMahon, the first to drink, were sickened, and Thom told the others to drink sparingly. In the middle of the night it rained, and someone suggested moving into the underbrush and licking water off the leaves. Ross and McMahon kept contact at first by touching feet as they licked. Somehow they got separated, and, being uncertain whether there were any Japs on the island, they became frightened. McMahon, trying to make his way back to the beach, bumped into someone and froze. It turned out to be Johnston, licking leaves on his own. In the morning the group saw that all the leaves were covered with droppings. Bitterly, they named the place Bird Island.

On this fourth day, the men were low. Even Johnston was low. He had changed his mind about praying. McGuire had a rosary around his neck, and Johnston said, "McGuire, give that necklace a working over." McGuire said quietly, "Yes, I'll take care of all you fellows." Kennedy was still unwilling to admit that things were hopeless. He asked Ross if he would swim with him to an island called Naru, to the southeast and even nearer Ferguson Passage. They were very weak indeed by now, but after an hour's swim they made it.

They walked painfully across Naru to the Ferguson Passage side, where they saw a Japanese barge aground on the reef. There were two men by the barge—possibly Japs. They apparently spotted Kennedy and Ross, for they got into a dugout canoe and hurriedly paddled to the other side of the

island. Kennedy and Ross moved up the beach.
They came upon an unopened rope-bound box and,
back in the trees, a little shelter containing a keg
of water, a Japanese gas mask, and a crude wooden
fetish shaped like a fish. There were Japanese hardtack and candy in the box and the two had a wary
feast. Down by the water they found a one-man
canoe. They hid from imagined Japs all day. When
night fell, Kennedy left Ross and took the canoe,
with some hardtack and a can of water from the
keg, out into Ferguson Passage. But no PT's came,
so he paddled to Bird Island. The men there told
him that the two men he had spotted by the barge
that morning were natives, who had paddled to
Bird Island. The natives had said that there were
Japs on Naru and the men had given Kennedy and
Ross up for lost. Then the natives had gone away.
Kennedy gave out small rations of crackers and
water, and the men went to sleep. During the night,
one man, who kept himself awake until the rest
were asleep, drank all the water in the can Kennedy had brought back. In the morning the others
figured out which was the guilty one. They swore
at him and found it hard to forgive him.

Before dawn, Kennedy started out in the canoe
to rejoin Ross on Naru, but when day broke a wind

arose and the canoe was swamped. Some natives appeared from nowhere in a canoe, rescued Kennedy, and took him to Naru. There they showed him where a two-man canoe was cached. Kennedy picked up a coconut with a smooth shell and scratched a message on it with a jackknife: "ELEVEN ALIVE NATIVE KNOWS POSIT AND REEFS NAURO ISLAND KENNEDY." Then he said to the natives, "Rendova, Rendova."

One of the natives seemed to understand. They took the coconut and paddled off.

Ross and Kennedy lay in a sickly daze all day. Toward evening it rained and they crawled under a bush. When it got dark, conscience took hold of Kennedy and he persuaded Ross to go out into Ferguson Passage with him in the two-man canoe. Ross argued against it. Kennedy insisted. The two started out in the canoe. They had shaped paddles from the boards of the Japanese box, and they took a coconut shell to bail with. As they got out into the Passage, the wind rose again and the water became choppy. The canoe began to fill. Ross bailed and Kennedy kept the bow into the wind. The waves grew until they were five or six feet high. Kennedy shouted, "Better turn around and go back!" As soon as the canoe was broadside to the waves, the water poured in and the dugout was swamped. The two clung to it, Kennedy at the bow, Ross at the stern. The tide carried them southward toward the open sea, so they kicked and tugged the canoe, aiming northwest. They struggled that way for two hours, not knowing whether they would hit the small island or drift into the endless open.

The weather got worse; rain poured down and they couldn't see more than ten feet. Kennedy shouted, "Sorry I got you out here, Barney!" Ross shouted back, "This would be a great time to say I told you so, but I won't!"

Soon the two could see a white line ahead and could hear a frightening roar—waves crashing on a reef. They had got out of the tidal current and were approaching the island all right, but now they realized that the wind and the waves were carrying them toward the reef. But it was too late to do anything, now that their canoe was swamped, except hang on and wait.

When they were near the reef, a wave broke Kennedy's hold, ripped him away from the canoe, turned him head over heels, and spun him in a violent rush. His ears roared and his eyes pinwheeled, and for the third time since the collision he thought he was dying. Somehow he was not thrown against the coral but floated into a kind of eddy. Suddenly he felt the reef under his feet. Steadying himself so that he would not be swept off it, he shouted, "Barney!" There was no reply. Kennedy thought of how he had insisted on going out in the canoe, and he screamed, "Barney!" This time Ross answered. He, too, had been thrown on the reef. He had not been as lucky as Kennedy; his right arm and shoulder had been cruelly lacerated by the coral, and his feet, which were already infected from earlier wounds, were cut some more.

The procession of Kennedy and Ross from reef to beach was a crazy one. Ross's feet hurt so much that Kennedy would hold one paddle on the bottom while Ross put a foot on it, then the other paddle forward for another step, then the first paddle forward again, until they reached sand. They fell on the beach and slept.

Kennedy and Ross were awakened early in the morning by a noise. They looked up and saw four husky natives. One walked up to them and said in an excellent English accent, "I have a letter for you, sir." Kennedy tore the note open. It said, "On His Majesty's Service. To the Senior Officer, Naru Island. I have just learned of your presence on Naru Is. I am in command of a New Zealand infantry

23

patrol operating in conjunction with U.S. Army troops on New Georgia. I strongly advise that you come with these natives to me. Meanwhile I shall be in radio communication with your authorities at Rendova, and we can finalize plans to collect balance of your party. Lt. Wincote. P. S. Will warn aviation of your crossing Ferguson Passage." [1]

Everyone shook hands and the four natives took Ross and Kennedy in their war canoe across to Bird Island to tell the others the good news. There the natives broke out a spirit stove and cooked a feast of yams and C ration. Then they built a lean-to for McMahon, whose burns had begun to rot and stink, and for Ross, whose arm had swelled to the size of a thigh because of the coral cuts. The natives put Kennedy in the bottom of their canoe and covered him with sacking and palm fronds, in case Japanese planes should buzz them. The long

[1] The wording and signature of this message are as Kennedy gave them to me in Boston in 1944. The message was in fact slightly, though not substantially, different; and many years later, after Kennedy had become President, the identity of the actual signer was uncovered — A. Reginald Evans. Wherever the name Wincote appears in the rest of this story, the reader will understand that that of Lieutenant Evans should be substituted.

trip was fun for the natives. They stopped once to try to grab a turtle, and laughed at the sport they were having. Thirty Japanese planes went over low toward Rendova, and the natives waved and shouted gaily. They rowed with a strange rhythm, pounding paddles on the gunwales between strokes. At last they reached a censored place. Lieutenant Wincote came to the water's edge and said formally, "How do you do. Leftenant Wincote."

Kennedy said, "Hello. I'm Kennedy."

Wincote said, "Come up to my tent and have a cup of tea."

In the middle of the night, after several radio conversations between Wincote's outfit and the PT base, Kennedy sat in the war canoe waiting at an arranged rendezvous for a PT. The moon went down at eleven-twenty. Shortly afterward Kennedy heard the signal he was waiting for—four shots. Kennedy fired four answering shots.

A voice shouted to him, "Hey, Jack!"

Kennedy said, "Where the hell you been?"

The voice said, "We got some food for you."

Kennedy said bitterly, "No, thanks, I just had a coconut."

A moment later a PT came alongside. Kennedy

jumped onto it and hugged the men aboard—his friends. In the American tradition, Kennedy held under his arm a couple of souvenirs: one of the improvised paddles and the Japanese gas mask.

With the help of the natives, the PT made its way to Bird Island. A skiff went in and picked up the men. In the deep of the night, the PT and its happy cargo roared back toward base. The squadron medic had sent some brandy along to revive the weakened men. Johnston felt the need of a little revival. In fact, he felt he needed quite a bit of revival. After taking care of that, he retired topside and sat with his arms around a couple of roly-poly, mission-trained natives. And in the fresh breeze on the way home they sang together a hymn all three happened to know:

> *Jesus loves me, this I know,*
> *For the Bible tells me so;*
> *Little ones to him belong,*
> *They are weak, but He is strong.*
> *Yes, Jesus loves me; yes, Jesus loves me . . .*

THE BATTLE OF THE RIVER

On October 8, in the first year of World War II,
I went down into a valley on Guadalcanal Island,
in the southwest Pacific, with Captain Charles
Rigaud of the United States Marines. A small
skirmish took place down there.

The skirmish was just an episode in an insignifi-
cant battle. The whole battle, which lasted three
days, did not bring as much reward to our arms
as several other battles on that island and elsewhere
did; but it illustrated how war has felt to men
everywhere.

The three-day action was called the Third Battle
of the Matanikau River. Few Americans have heard
of the Matanikau River, to say nothing of its Third
Battle. The river is a light brown stream winding
through a jungle valley about five miles west of
the precarious footing the Marines held at Henderson Field. When I arrived on Guadalcanal, our
forces did not hold positions out to the Matanikau.
The Japanese were moving up in some strength,
evidently to try to establish a bridgehead over the
river—the first in a series of heavy moves against

our camp. It became imperative for our troops to push to the river and force the enemy back beyond it, before it was too late.

The first two battles of the Matanikau River had been earlier attempts to do just that. In the first one, the Marines tried to do the job frontally, but their force was too small. In the second, they tried a tactic of encirclement, but again not enough men were thrown into action. The third time, with the enemy constantly growing in strength, there could be no question of failing.

"Awright! Reveille! It's six o'clock. Come on, fellas, all out. Reveille!"

Although it was just barely light, it did not take much persuasion to start the men in Colonel Amor Leroy Sims's camp stirring. They wandered out to brush their teeth, to shave, to start cramming things into their packs, to polish their already polished rifles.

Word was passed up through the encampment: "Mass at six-thirty for those who want it. Six-thirty mass." Attendance was pretty good that morning. While that religious rite was being carried out, there was also a pagan touch. Four buzzards flew over the camp. "To the right hand," said a young Marine, like a Roman sage. "Our fortunes will be good."

One of the last orders we had heard Colonel Sims give the evening before was to the officer of the mess: "Breakfast in the morning must be a good, solid, hot meal. And if we get back from starving ourselves for two or three days out there and find that you fellows who stay behind have been gourmandizing, someone'll be shot at dawn."

Breakfast was solid, all right—our last square meal for three days. On the table there were huge pans full of sliced pineapples, beans, creamed chipped beef, a rice-and-raisin stew, crackers, canned butter, jam, and coffee.

As the units began lining up to move out, the first artillery barrage broke out—our guns coughing deeply, and then a minute later the answering coughs, far out. At eight-thirty the column started to move. We had a good long hike ahead of us. Colonel Sims's encampment was about eight miles from the Matanikau, but terrain would force the column to move at least fifteen miles before contact.

Gradually the column fell into silence. The walking, which had been casual and purposely out of step, began to get stiffer and more formal, and finally much of the column was in step. On the engineers' crudely bulldozed roadway, there began to be a regular *crunch-crunch-crunch* that reminded me of all the newsreels I had seen of feet parading on asphalt, to a background of cheering and band music. As a matter of fact, we had a band with us, but the bandsmen were equipped with first-aid stuff, stretchers, and rifles.

For a time the column wound through thick jungle, then emerged on a grassy plain edged by a kind of Great Wall of steep, bare ridges. Just before we reached the first of the ridges, Colonel Sims turned in his position at the head of the column and said, "Ten-minute break. Get off the road, spread right out."

Lieutenant Colonel Julian Frisbie, Colonel Sims's hulking executive officer, sat cross-legged in the grass and thundered at me, "Would you like to hear about our plan of operation?

"It's a very simple scheme," he explained. "We know that the Japs have moved up into positions on the other side of the mouth of the Matanikau. Perhaps some of them have already crossed to this side. Our aim is to cut off and kill or capture as many as we can. Those which we don't pocket we must drive back.

"Edson—that's Colonel Merritt Edson, who trained the first Marine raiders—will push a holding attack to the river right at the mouth, and try to make the Japs think we intend to force a crossing there. Whaling actually will force a crossing quite a little higher up, and then will wheel downstream beside the river. Hanneken will lead part of our force through behind Whaling, will go deeper than Whaling, and then cut right. Then Puller will go through deeper yet and cut right, too. If necessary another force will go around by sea in Higgins boats and land behind the Japs to close the trap.

"This is very much like the plan Lee used at the

31

Chickahominy, when he had Magruder make a demonstration south of the river, and sent D. H. Hill, A. P. Hill, and Longstreet across at successive bridges, with Jackson closing the trap at the rear. We aren't sending the units in with quite the same pattern, but it's the same general idea. The advantage of our scheme is that Whaling goes in, and if he finds the going impossible, we haven't yet committed Hanneken and Puller, and we can revise our tactics. I think it'll work."

"All up! Let's go!"

The column started sluggishly up again. As it wound up over the ridges, past a battery of 75's through a gap in the double-apron barbed-wire barrier, and out into the beginnings of no man's land, it looked less like a drill-ground army than like a band of western pioneers, wary of Indians. Each man was armed to his own taste and heart's content. Most carried rugged old 1903 bolt-action Springfields. A few had Browning automatic rifles. Almost all carried knives, slung from their belts, fastened to their packs, or strapped to their legs. Several had field shovels. Many carried pistols. Pockets bulged with grenades. Some were not satisfied with one bayonet, but carried two. There were even a couple of Jap swords. But probably the greatest refinement was a weapon I spotted in the tunic pocket of Corporal Joseph Gagney, of Augusta, Maine—a twelve-inch screwdriver.

I asked him how he happened to bring that along.

"Oh," he said, "just found it on my person."

"When do you expect to use it?"

"Never can tell, might lose my bayonet with some Japs in the neighborhood."

After we came out on the last and highest ridge, Colonel Sims and I walked by a short cut down to a coastwise road, where we commandeered a jeep and rode forward as far as we could. This coast sector was where Colonel Edson, past master of the bush, was staging his holding attack. We asked our way to his command post.

Colonel Edson was not a fierce Marine. In fact, he appeared almost shy. Yet he was probably then among the five finest combat commanders in all the U.S. Armed Forces. "I hope the Japs will have some respect for American fighting men after this campaign," he says so quietly you have to lean forward to catch it all. "I certainly have learned respect for the Japs. What they have done is to take Indian warfare and apply it to the twentieth century. They use all the Indian tricks to demoralize their enemy. They're good, all right, but"—Colonel Edson's voice

33

trails off into an embarrassed whisper—"I think we're better."

Edson's forward command post stood in the last of the palm trees, and consisted of a foxhole and a field telephone slung on a coconut tree. As we came up, he was sitting on the ground, cross-legged, talking to one of his units on the phone.

When he was through phoning, Sims asked him what his situation was. "Only slight contact so far," he said. "We've met about a company of Japs on this side of the river, and they seem to be pretty well placed."

"I hope the muzzlers aren't pulling back," Sims said.

"Don't think so. They seem to have some mortars on the other side of the river, and I think they're pretty solid over there."

Here at Edson's C.P. I heard for the first time close at hand the tight-woven noise of war. The constant fabric of the noise was rifle fire. Like a knife tearing into the fabric, every once in a while there would be a short burst of machine-gun fire. Forward we could hear bombs falling into the jungle, and the chatter of strafing P-39's. A mortar battery directly in front of us was doubly noisy, for its commander was an old-fashioned hollering

Marine. But weirdest of all was the sound of our artillery shells passing overhead. At this angle, probably just about under the zenith of their trajectory, they gave off a soft, fluttery sound, like that of a man blowing through a keyhole.

I inquired about the doubly noisy mortar battery. It belonged, I was told, to a character such as you would find only in the Marine Corps. This was Master Gunner Sergeant Lou Diamond, who was said to be approximately two hundred years old. I saw him presently, a giant with a full gray beard, an admirable paunch, and the bearing of a man daring you to insult him. Lou was so old that there was some question whether to take him along on such a hazardous job as the Solomons campaign. He was getting too unwieldy to clamber up and down cargo nets. On one of the last days before embarking, Lou found out that they were debating about his antiquity, so he went out and directed loading operations with such vehemence that for a time he lost his voice entirely; the next morning he was told he could go along.

Now there he was, proving that even if he out-Methuselahed Methuselah, he would still be the best damn mortar man in the Marines. As he went by he was, as usual, out of patience. He wanted to

keep on firing, and had been told to hold back.
"Wait and wait and wait and wait," he roared.
"Some people around here'll fall on their arse from
waiting. . . ."

For the next two hours and more we were to
witness some waiting which was nearly disastrous
to the general plan. This delay was caused by the
watering of our force. The men had hiked more
than ten miles under a broiling sun, and most had
emptied their canteens. No one was certain when
there would be another chance to water up—and
water is the most precious commodity in human
endurance. Therefore it was extremely important
for the men to fill up.

The disaster was the way they did it. The water
source was a big trailer tank, which had been
towed out from the camp by a truck. The tank had
only one faucet, and each man had to file by, turn
the faucet on, hold his canteen under it, and turn
it off again. This took time, far too much time.

We turned off the beach road and cut up through
a jungle defile parallel to the Matanikau. Now we
were really moving into position, and word was
passed that we must be on the lookout for snipers.
The trail led us constantly upward. Occasionally
we would break out onto a grassy knoll, then plunge

back into the jungle. The jungle seemed alien, an almost poisonous place. It closed in tightly on either side of the trail, a tangle of nameless vines and trees.

By midafternoon our column had emerged on the crest of a broad and fairly high ridge, which looked down over the whole area of battle. It was there that I came to understand the expression, "the fog of war." We thought we knew where we were, then found we didn't, then found it wasn't too easy to locate ourselves. The Matanikau was hidden from our view by intervening ridges, so we were not sure of its course.

Fortunately we were high enough to see the coastline; we could figure out where we were by triangulation. One of the men took a bearing with a little field compass on Point Cruz, off to our left. Then he took a bearing on Lunga Point, back where the camp lay. He drew the two lines of bearing on the map, tangent to the tips of the points—and where the lines crossed was our position.

Lieutenant Colonel Puller's men were following us up the trail. When Sims found where we were, he told Puller that we would have to push on, even though darkness might shut down before we

37

reached the prearranged bivouac. Now Colonel Puller was one of the hardest Marine officers to restrain, once he got started. He was as proud of his men as they were of him. And so when Colonel Sims told him to move on, he threw out his chest, blew out his cheeks, and said, "That's fine. Couldn't be better. My men are prepared to spend the night right on the trail. And that's the best place to be if you want to move anywhere."

Colonel Frisbie overheard this and couldn't resist giving The Puller a rib. "Gwan," he said, "we know your men are tough. The trouble with the trails along these ridges is that there's not enough horse dung for your men to use as pillows."

As we moved forward, the high flat snap of Jap snipers' rifles became more and more frequent. Once in a while, from nowhere, a lone bullet would sing over our heads like a supercharged bee, and hundreds of men would involuntarily duck, even though the bullet was long past. The worst seemed to come from a valley ahead and to the left of us. Down there Whaling was trying to force his way through to the river, and his men were meeting not only sniper fire but occasional machine-gun and mortar fire. When I looked at the faces of a handful of Colonel Sims's young men, who by now were already friends of mine—C. B., Bill, Ralph, Irving, Ted—I saw that they were no longer boastful joking lads. The music in that valley made them almost elderly.

Our bivouac for the night was on a ridge right above that valley, and we had hardly had time to set up some radio equipment and to get the field telephone working when the walking wounded began to dribble up the awful incline out of the valley: young fellows with bandages wrapped scarflike around their necks, or with arms in slings, or with shirts off and huge red-and-white patches on their chests. They struggled silently up that forty-five-degree slope, absolutely silent about what they had seen and how they felt, most with a cigarette dangling lifelessly, perhaps unlit, out of one corner of the mouth, their eyes varnished over with pain.

Near the equator, the sun rises at about six and sets at about six all year round. By a quarter past six that night, it was nearly dark. An overcast was settling down; it looked like rain.

Breakfast had been huge, but we had done quite a bit of work in twelve hours. We were famished. There were no niceties out here; no please-pass-the-salt and no sir-may-I-please-be-excused. We just flopped down wherever we happened to be and

39

opened our rations and gulped them down. The main course was Ration C—fifteen ounces of meat-and-vegetable hash, straight from the can, cold but delicious that evening. For dessert we had a bar of Ration D.

Gradually our bivouac settled down for the night. The men snuggled down into whatever comfortable spots they could find. They couldn't find many, because Guadalcanal's ridges came up, once upon a time, out of the sea, and their composition is nine-tenths crumbled coral—not the stuff of beauty rest.

C.B. had had the sense, as I had not, to look for a comfortable bed before it got pitch dark. The spot he picked was at the military crest—not on top of the ridge, but a little down the side—so we would not be silhouetted at dawn, and so sniper fire from the opposite side of the ridge could not reach us. Somehow he had found a place about twelve feet long and six feet wide where the coral was quite finely crumbled. When he heard me stumbling around and cursing coral, he called me over. I took off my pack and my canteen, folded my poncho double, and settled down. There was nothing to serve as pillow except either my pack, which was full of ration cans, or my steel helmet. I finally found that the most comfortable arrangement was to put my helmet on, and let it contend with the coral.

"Well, what do you think of the Marines?" C.B. asked.

I told him I was sold.

"They're a pretty fine bunch," he said. "Lots of this particular gang are pretty green, but they're willing and bright. There's no griping among the privates in the Marine Corps for two reasons. The first is that they're all volunteers. If one of them starts talking back, the officer says, 'Nobody drafted you, Mac,' and every time, the squawker stops squawking. The other thing is that these men are a really high type. In peacetime the Corps only accepted about twenty per cent of the applicants. In fact, the only difference between our officers and our privates is luck. One fellow got a break that the other didn't happen to get, and so he has the advantage of position."

And suddenly, like a child falling off in the middle of a bedtime story, C.B. was breathing hard and regularly. From then on, the night was in my hands, and I didn't like it.

My bedroom was the hollow, empty sky, and every once in a while a 105-mm. shell would scream in one window and out the other. There was nothing

41

soft and fluffy about the noise here. We lay within two hundred yards of where the shells were landing, and we heard the peculiar drilling sound you get only on the receiving end of artillery fire. All through the night snipers took pot shots at the ridges.

It was five in the morning before I dropped off. At five-thirty it started raining, and I waked up again. So did all the Marines. The poncho helped, but rain infiltrates better than the Japs. Soon a spot here, a patch there, got wet. With the damp came chills, and before long there were a lot of miserable Marines. The only consolation was that across the way there were undoubtedly a lot of miserable Japs.

War is nine-tenths waiting—waiting in line for chow, waiting for promotion, waiting for mail, for an air raid, for dawn, for reinforcements, for orders, for the men in the front to move, for relief. All that morning, while time seemed so important to a layman, we waited. The plan was for Whaling to force his crossing, after which Sims's men, under Hanneken and Puller, would follow through.

The artillery and plane barrage that morning was a grim show from our grandstand ridge. The climax of the show was when two TBF's, the Navy's most graceful planes, came over and dropped two strings of hundred-pound bombs. From our ridge we could see the bombs leave their bays, describe their parabola, and fall, terribly, where they were intended to fall. All along our ridge and the next, the Marines stood up and cheered.

When the barrage subsided, huge white birds circled in terror over the jungle across the way, and we had visions of the Japs circling in terror underneath. Bill, evidently thinking of them, said quietly, "War is nice, but peace is nicer."

We settled down to wait for Whaling to have success. A few of us crept out on a knoll which towered above the river itself; we could look down on the area where Whaling's men were doing their bitter work, and we could hear the chatter of their guns, but we could see no movement, so dense was the growth. In midmorning we did see seven Japs running away up a burnt-off ridge across from us. A machine gun about twenty feet from us snapped at their heels, and they dived for cover. "How did you like the sound of that gun?" crowed one of the gunners. "That's the best damn gun in the regiment—in the Corps, for that matter."

At 11:40 A.M. the first of Whaling's men appeared on the ridges across the river. A signalman semaphored back the identification of the unit, so we would not fire on them. At 11:45 Whaling sent a message back that the crossing had been secured. Colonel Hanneken's men began to move. It was time for me to join a unit and go down.

Captain Charles Alfred Rigaud, standing there in the drizzle about to lead his heavy machine-gun company forward, looked like anything except a killer who took no prisoners. He had a boy's face. There were large, dark circles of weariness and worry under his eyes. His mustache was not quite convincing.

We stood on a high grassy ridge above a three-hundred-foot cliff. In the valley below was a little stream, which ran into the Matanikau River. Captain Rigaud's mission was to clear the valley of snipers, push to the river, and force a crossing.

The crossing was supposed to be made easy by the fact that Whaling's force was working around behind the Japs on the other side of the river, so the enemy would be trapped. But Whaling had run into trouble and been delayed. Therefore Captain Rigaud's mission was doomed before it started—but he had no way of knowing that.

I asked Captain Rigaud if I could go along with him. "You may go if you want to," he said, as if any-

one who would want to was crazy. My valor was
certainly of ignorance: if I had any understanding
of what Company H might meet, I never would
have gone along.

This was a company of veterans. They had been
in every battle so far, and except perhaps for Edson's Raiders, had been in all the toughest spots.
The company had already lost twenty-two dead.
They were tired; they had been on Guadalcanal two
months. They were sure of themselves but surfeited
with fighting.

We went down into the valley in single file. My
position in line was immediately behind Captain
Rigaud. About half the company was ahead of us,
about half behind. The company's proper weapons
were heavy machine guns, which the men carried
broken down. Quite a few of the men carried ammunition boxes in both hands—a terrible load in
such country. Some had rifles. Captain Rigaud and
some of his platoon leaders had Browning automatic
rifles.

After we had forded the stream once, the jungle
suddenly became stiflingly thick. This was enemy
territory in earnest. Our column moved in absolute
silence. Captain Rigaud whispered to the man in
front of him and to me that we should pass the word

along for men to keep five paces apart, so as not to give snipers bunched targets. The message hissed forward and backward along the line in a whisper: "Keep five paces . . . keep five paces . . . keep five paces . . ."

It is impossible to describe the creepy sensation of walking through that empty-looking but crowded-seeming jungle. Parakeets and cockatoos screeched from nowhere. There was one bird with an altogether unmusical call which sounded exactly like a man whistling shrilly through his fingers three times —and then another, far off in Jap territory, would answer.

As we sneaked forward, the feeling of tenseness steadily increased. The next word to be passed back from the head of the line came slowly, in whispers, for it was a long message: "Keep sharp lookout to right and to left . . . keep sharp lookout to right and to left . . . keep sharp lookout to right and to left . . ."

As if we had to be told! After this word, another kind of message came back along the line: the tiny clicks of bullets being slipped into the chambers of weapons.

It was probably because I was a bad soldier, and looked at the ground rather than up in the trees, that I stumbled on my first really tangible evidence of the enemy. To the left of the trail, at the foot of a huge tree, I found a green head net. It was small, and was made like some little minnow net. I picked it up, touched Captain Rigaud on the arm, and showed it to him.

Without changing his expression, he nodded, and shaped the soundless word, "Jap," with his lips. Belatedly, it occurred to me to look up in the tree. There was nothing.

A little farther along, I noticed a rifle lying in the stream. It had a short stock and a long barrel—not like any U.S. type I had seen. Again I touched Captain Rigaud's arm and pointed. He nodded again and shaped the same word: "Jap."

We were moving very slowly now. It seemed strange to me to be walking erect. I had had visions of men in the jungle slithering along on their bellies, or at least creeping on all fours, like animals. But we didn't even stoop.

Up ahead, suddenly, three or four rifle shots—the high-pitched Jap kind—broke the silence. Almost at once a message came cantering back along the line: "Hold it up . . . hold it up . . . hold it up . . ."

A strange little conversation followed. Several of

us were bunched together waiting to move—Captain Rigaud, Peppard, Calder, Brizzard. Suddenly one of them whispered, "Hey, what I'd give for a piece of blueberry pie!"

Another whispered, "Personally I prefer mince."

A third whispered, "Make mine apple with a few raisins in it and lots of cinnamon: you know, southern style."

The line started moving again without any more shots having been fired and without the passing of an order. Now we knew definitely that there were snipers ahead, and all along the line there were anxious upturned faces.

About a hundred yards farther along, I got a real shock. I had been looking upward along with the rest when suddenly right by my feet to the left of the trail I saw a dead Marine. Captain Rigaud glanced back at me. His lips did not shape any word this time, but his bitter young face said, as plainly as if he had shouted it, "The Japs are ——s."

We kept on moving, crossing and recrossing the stream, which grew wider and more sluggish. We were apparently nearing the Matanikau. Up ahead, as a matter of fact, some of the men had already crossed the river. There seemed to be no opposition;

we had reason to hope that Whaling had already
cleaned out whatever had been on the other side,
and that our job would be a pushover. Just a sniper
or two to hunt down and kill.

The captain and I were about seventy-five feet
from the river when he found out how wrong our
hope was.

The signal was a single shot from a sniper. A
couple of seconds after it, snipers all around started
to fire on us. Machine guns from across the river
began to shoot. But the terrible thing was that Jap
mortars over there opened up, too.

The Japs had made their calculations perfectly.
There were only three or four natural crossings of
the river; this was one of them. And so they had set
their trap. They had machine guns all mounted,
ready to pour stuff into the jungle bottleneck at the
stream's junction with the river. They had snipers
scattered on both sides of the river. And they had
their mortars all set to lob deadly explosions into
the same area. Their plan had been to hold their
fire and let the enemy get well into the trap before
snapping it, and this they had done with too much
success.

Had we been infantry, the trap might not have

49

worked. Brave men with rifles and grenades could have wiped out the enemy nests. Captain Rigaud's helplessness was that he could not bring his weapons to bear. Heavy machine guns take some time to be assembled and mounted. In that narrow defile his men, as brave as any, never succeeded in getting more than two guns firing.

The mortar fire was what was terrifying. Beside it, the Japs' sniper fire and even machine-gun fire, with its soprano, small-sounding reports, seemed a mere botheration. But each explosion of mortar fire was a word spoken by death.

When the first bolts of this awful thunder began to fall among Rigaud's men, we hit the ground. We were like earthy insects with some great foot being set down in our midst, and we scurried for little crannies—cavities under the roots of huge trees, little gullies, dead logs. Explosions were about ten seconds apart, and all around us, now fifty yards away, now twenty feet. And all the while snipers and machine gunners wrote in their nasty punctuation. Our own guns answered from time to time, but not enough.

Individually the Marines in that outfit were as brave as any fighters in any army in the world. But when fear began to be epidemic in that closed-in place, no one was immune; no one could resist it.

The Marines had been deeply enough indoctrinated so that even flight did not wipe out the formulas, and soon the word came whispered back: "Withdraw . . . withdraw . . . withdraw . . ."

Then they started moving back, slowly at first, then running wildly.

It was then that Charles Alfred Rigaud, the boy with tired circles under his eyes, showed himself to be a good officer and grown man. Despite the snipers all around us, despite the machine guns and the mortars, he stood right up on his feet and shouted out, "Who in ——'s name gave that order?"

This was enough to freeze the men in their tracks.

Next, by a combination of blistering sarcasm, orders, and cajolery, he not only got the men back into position; he got them in a mood to fight again. I am certain that all along, Captain Rigaud was just as terrified as the rest of us were, for he was eminently human. But I kept quite close to Captain Rigaud, and I could not see a single tremor of his hands. If I had, I would have attributed it to anger.

When he had put his men back into position, he immediately made preparations to get them out in an orderly fashion. He could see that the position was untenable; staying there would merely mean

51

losing dozens of men who could live to fight successfully another day. He could not get his weapons into play; obviously Whaling's force had not unsettled the enemy across the river. Therefore he beckoned to a runner, filled out a request for permission to withdraw on his yellow message pad, sent the runner off to the rear C.P., and then set about passing whispered orders for the withdrawal.

Now the heroism of the medical corpsmen and bandsmen showed itself. They went into the worst places and began moving the wounded. I joined them because, I guess, I just thought that was the fastest way to get the hell out of there.

I attached myself to a group who were wounded in a dreadful way. They had no open wounds; they shed no blood; they seemed merely to have been attacked by some mysterious germ of war that made them groan, hold their sides, limp, and stagger. They were shock and blast victims.

There were not enough corpsmen to assist more than the unconscious and leg-wounded men, so they had set these dazed men to helping each other. It was like the blind leading the blind. I commandeered three unhurt privates, and we began to half-carry, half-drag the worst of these strange casualties.

The rain and trampling had made the trail so bad now that a sound man walking alone would occasionally fall, and in some steep places would have to crawl on hands and knees, pulling himself by exposed roots and leaning bamboo trunks. We slid, crept, walked, wallowed, waded, and staggered, like drunken men. One man kept striking the sides of his befuddled skull with his fists. Another kept his hands over his ears. Several had badly battered legs, and behaved like football players with excruciating Charley horses.

The worst blast victim, who kept himself conscious only by his guts, was a boy whom I shall call Charley Utley. Part of the time we had to carry him, part of the time he could drag his feet along while I supported him. Before we went very far, a corpsman, who saw what pain he was in, injected some morphine in his arm. Utley had a caved-in chest, and one of his legs was bruised almost beyond use.

As we struggled along the trail he kept asking for his sergeant, Bauer. "Don't leave Bauer," the wounded boy pleaded.

Gradually I pieced together what had happened. Utley and several of these others had been the crew of one of the machine guns that did get into action. Sergeant Bauer was in command of the gun. While

53

they were approach-firing, a mortar grenade went off near them, knocking the crew all over the place. Most of the men took cover. But Bauer crawled back to the gun just in time for another grenade to come much closer yet.

We asked around in the group to see if Bauer was with us, but he was not. "They got him sure," one said.

"He shouldn't have gone back," Utley said. "Why in hell did he have to go back?"

All the way out of that valley of the shadow, Charley Utley mumbled about his friend Sergeant Bauer.

The farther we went, the harder the going seemed to be. We all became tired, and the hurt men slowed down considerably. There were some steep places where we had to sit Utley down in the mud and slide him down ten feet to the stream; in other places, uphill, we had to form a chain of hands and work him up very slowly.

It was almost dark when we got out of the jungle, and by the time we had negotiated the last steep ridge, it was hard to tell the difference between the wounded men and the bearers. We turned the wounded over to Doc New, the Navy surgeon, who had an emergency dressing station set up on the crest of the last ridge.

While I talked with Captain Rigaud, who had led his men out by a shorter way and had beaten us in, corpsmen and bandsmen hurried down for Bauer. It was pitch dark when they found him. They were in territory, remember, where snipers had been all around, and where, if they betrayed themselves by the slightest sound, they might have mortar fire pouring down on them.

One of the bandsmen asked Bauer, "How you feel, Mac?"

He said, "I think I can make it."

The men fashioned a stretcher out of two rifles and a poncho, and started out. Bauer was in bad shape. He was conscious, but that was about all.

The only way the group could find their path was to follow, hand over hand, a telephone wire which some wire stringer had carried down into that hot valley. In the darkness they had great difficulty making progress, and had to halt for long rests.

Men who are wounded do not talk rhetorically; famous last words are usually edited after the fact. Bauer's sentences to Sergeant Lewis Isaak and Private Clinton Prater were simple requests: "Help me sit up, will you please. Oh God, my stomach." . . . Soon he said very softly, "No, no, I've got to lie down, do it slow." They eased him down. For a few minutes his head tossed quickly from side to side.

He gave a few short breaths and then just stopped breathing.

A dying officer was brought to Doc New. He was in absolute shock. He was gray as ashes in the face. His hands were cold. You could not feel his pulse. He had suffered a bad wound from mortar shrapnel in his left knee, and he had another shrapnel wound in his right hand. Doc New realized that blood plasma, and lots of it, was all that could save this man.

The doctor had to maintain blackout, and he had also to try to keep the man warm. To serve both these ends, most of his corpsmen gave up their ponchos. Working feverishly, interposing rustic expressions—"Dadgummit" and "Gollydingwhiz"—he covered first the wounded man, then his own head and shoulders, with ponchos. Before the first unit of 250 cc. of plasma was in the wounded man's veins, the patient came out of his coma. By the time the second was in, he was able to speak. By morning he was able to talk to his C.P. on a field phone, stand the ride on a stretcher down to the beach road, and sit up in a jeep on the way back to the camp hospital.

The Battle of the River

The sunrise next morning, after the slop and terror of the day before, was one of the most beautiful things a lot of Marines had ever seen. Bill said, "Anyone who can't see beauty in that doesn't deserve to live. My mother would like to see that. 'Dear Mom: You should've seen the sunrise this morning.' . . ."

Operations now proceeded according to plan—the formal way of saying, "with moderate but unspectacular success." By 10:20 A.M. the leading troops of the flanking units had reached the beach. They found that most of the Japs had withdrawn during the night, taking their wounded with them. Evidently they had pulled out in quite a hurry, for they had left packs and other equipment behind. They left two hundred dead on the field. The Marines lost sixty dead—their worst casualties in any single operation on Guadalcanal up to that time.

Probably the bitterest clash of the whole battle had occurred at the mouth of the Matanikau. For the two whole days, Edson had been unable to root out the entrenched company of Japs on the east side of the river. Finally, on the second night, he called on his Raiders. He put them between the Japs and the spit, their only avenue of escape.

In the pitch-black night the Japs made a desperate

break. They put on a shrieking attack into the Raiders' positions. Some of them leaped silently into foxholes beside the Marines, who had no way of knowing whether the intruders were comrades or enemy. In the knifework that followed, the Marines came out better than the Japs, to judge by the number of dead in the foxholes in the morning.

Now all that was behind the men. The air that morning was bland. On the hillside where Bill and C.B. were bivouacked, the sun beat down and warmed the Marines and melted away the cold thing that had settled hard inside them the afternoon and night before.

A few of them decided they would rather die than go any longer without some hot coffee. They scoured around for some dry wood and finally, at the upper edge of a coral precipice, found some little bushes that had been a season dead and weathered. They broke twigs up into tiny fragments about twice the size of matches. They lit up and found to their delight that the twigs burned with a light blue haze, which would not betray their position. One fellow who had not helped gather the twigs kept putting his canteen cup right over the best part of the fire, until one of the others snapped at him,

"Didn't you ever hear that old American custom, no work, no eat? Scram, Mac."

And so, returning to everyday actions and thoughts, the men did their best to forget the horrors of the battle of the river.

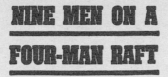

NINE MEN ON A
FOUR-MAN RAFT

During the month of September, 1942, I was a war correspondent aboard the U.S. aircraft carrier Hornet in the southwest Pacific. One day the carrier received a message that a destroyer in its screen had picked up seven men, the crew of a Flying Fortress, who had been found in a life raft in the sea. Presently the destroyer came alongside the Hornet, and the men were transferred to the carrier, where they were all put in sick bay. After they recovered their strength, they told me this story of their seven-day voyage on an inflated raft that had been designed to carry only four men.

I have put the entire story in the mouth of Lieutenant A. W. Anderson, the copilot, but parts of it came from Lieutenant J. P. Van Hour, the pilot, and other crew members.

B-17 Number 41-2404 was one of the oldest planes we had. Even before we got her, she was called "The Spider." We didn't know for a long time what the reason was, until we figured out it must have been because she was hanging by nothing but a thread. Still, we couldn't get rid of her. Every time another crew took her out, we used to wish that they would drop her in the drink. One day we went up and bombed Tulagi and some Zeros jumped all over us and knocked out two turrets, but they couldn't down her. She was tough. But we knew she'd go sometime.

Well, a day came when we were out, four ships of us, looking for Japs. "The Spider" was in the number-three position, and we had just swung around to return to our base when the inboard engine on the right side conked out. We couldn't keep up with the formation on the other three engines, and we kept dropping back.

When night settled down we lost all track of the formation and started flying blind. We knew we were somewhere over the New Hebrides Islands, but there was a lot of overcast and we didn't dare let down for fear of hitting a mountain. Occasionally we would run into giant thunderheads, where it took all the strength of both pilots to hold a true course.

Our estimated time of arrival was nine-thirty, and at that time we had not yet sighted the home island. We had about two hours' gas left, so we asked for bearing signals and turned on our radio compass; but its generator went out on us. We circled the vicinity of the home island for a long time, hoping to see a light. It soon became imperative that we land somewhere, as we had barely twenty minutes' gas supply left.

The crew was told to prepare for a water landing. We settled through the overcast, down, down; the overcast seemed never to end. We burst through at an altitude of only about one hundred feet, and we saw the waves, which were running uncomfortably high. We hit with a rending crash. It seemed as though the whole world was exploding around us.

I could look out the copilot's window and see the water rushing by. It occurred to me that I had neglected to open my escape window. With a sickening sensation I tugged at it, and by some miracle it hadn't jammed, so I made hasty use of it.

The one thing we had been told about going into the drink was that a B-17 would float only about thirty seconds, so we got out as fast as we could. Our plane floated all of two and a half minutes. We wish we had known she was going to, because we could have taken more things out of her than we did.

Nine Men on a Four-Man Raft

We attempted to free the life rafts that we were carrying—two four-man rafts and one two-man raft. One four-man raft jammed and couldn't be removed from its compartment in the fuselage. The other came out with only one side inflated, and the two-man raft was in the same condition. Someone swam over and got the emergency rations. We lashed the rafts together and put the rations in the big raft. It was too dark then to do anything further, so we simply hung on for dear life till morning.

FIRST DAY: This morning at sunup we surveyed our predicament. The men, on the whole, were in good condition—some nasty cuts and bruises but no broken bones. The enlisted men were in worse shape than the pilots, because they had been knocked around more severely when we landed. A couple of them had lost a lot of blood, so started with quite a handicap. However, our spirits were high because we fully expected to be picked up that day.

The large raft had a three-cornered rip in its bottom fabric, through which most of the rations had fallen. We still had one gallon of water, a few crackers, and ten candy bars, 1937 vintage, so ancient and stale they made one sick to look at them. The water hadn't been changed for so long that it had rotted the cork inside the canteen cap and had rusted the cap, and when we opened the container the stench nearly knocked us over. We weren't even sure it was water; we thought it might be kerosene or hydraulic fluid, because it was brown and smelled so strong. It was like something out of the radiator of a car after a long winter. Little did we know how good it would taste later on. We had a can of grape juice, but it was lost when the raft capsized later. We also had a can of tomato juice, but after we opened it and drank half, the other half spoiled. We also had one automatic pistol, a few flares, and two cans of aluminum slick.

We located a pump, fully inflated the two rafts, and put two men in the small one and seven in the larger. The water came up to our knees through the hole in the bottom of the larger raft; there was no way of patching the tear. About eleven-thirty we spotted a Navy PBY, a large search plane, coming over close. We fired four flares but received no response, and some of our high spirits faded as the plane disappeared over the horizon. However, we all cursed the pilot heartily and then felt better prepared to wait for the next one.

The seas grew higher toward nightfall. The small raft couldn't be kept afloat in them, so we deflated it, pushed it under the seats of the larger raft, and inflated it again. This increased our buoyancy, but we had nine men in a four-man boat, and this made it necessary for all hands to sit around the edges quietly, our feet in the center, like a flock of ducks on an inner tube. We couldn't sleep because if one man, falling asleep, should begin to topple, it would rock the raft badly. The waves swept over us all night, soaking every man and chilling him to the bone. The night wore on and on. After ages of cold and pain the sun rose to warm our bodies.

SECOND DAY: We cautiously stretched ourselves, relieving some of our cramps, and looked out over the horizon. Nothing was to be seen on any side but water and sky.

A curious sea gull slowly flew over the raft, pausing, as if in amazement at the sight we made, a few feet overhead. Sergeant R. P. Anderson, the radioman (no relation of mine), took careful aim with the pistol, but just as he fired the boat rocked. A clean miss. There were no condemnations; we were getting used to bad breaks.

The next one, though, was hard to take. Another plane flew up, seemingly straight toward us. It passed not more than a mile away. We could practically see the pilot's eyes. But it went on by.

We took our first bite of candy, one quarter of a bar, and washed it down with one sip of water. Even then the stuff tasted awful.

I rigged up a fishline with a piece of tinfoil as spinner. Late in the afternoon we had one strike, but we lost the fish at the boat's edge. We were beginning to find some hope in all the bad luck, because we were confident it had to improve sooner or later: the law of averages had to be on our side.

Night closed down again on nine weary, sleepless men, who endured cold and discomfort tenfold that of the preceding night. Corporal D'Amour became delirious, perhaps as a result of a blow on the head in our landing. Always a taciturn, conscientious man, he was now a big problem. We quieted him as much as possible.

THIRD DAY: D'Amour grew steadily worse today—physical condition apparently good but delirium mounting. He thought he was still flying, and he tried to stand up to climb into his turret and fix his gun, and we had to hold him so he wouldn't upset the boat. He would see whole droves of tanks and jeeps down there under the raft, and once he said, "Look at the B-17's!"

We all said, "Where? Where?"

He pointed down under the raft, and said, "Down there—don't you see them?"

The remainder of the crew were in fair shape. Everyone's feet had swollen to nearly twice normal size, with large salt-water sores beginning to show, but no one complained.

For want of something else to do, we sorted out our gear and cleaned it as well as we could. Then Sergeant Gagnon set to work fashioning a sail by fastening a shirt over two paddles. It wasn't too practical, but we had a stiff southwest wind, and Lieutenant Darden, our navigator, believed we could reach New Caledonia if we ran before it. We were ready to take any likely chance, so we acted on his suggestion.

Later Lieutenant Van Hour, the pilot, contrived a spinner from his expensive new wrist watch. We trolled with this all day but had no luck.

Toward noon Private Murray looked over the side and saw a shark that he claimed looked like the fuselage of a fighter plane, a P-40. It came closer, later on, and we could see it was an enormous tiger shark. We watched it nervously for some time, but apparently it was more curious than hungry. We took care not to tempt it too far. It edged over closer and closer, eventually coming within a few feet, then it rolled over slowly and with a thud hit the bottom of the boat, raking its huge body its full length. I grabbed the pistol and waited for the next pass, which wasn't long in coming. As he reached the boat, I put the gun about two feet from his head and fired. The water boiled for a minute as he took off for parts unknown. Later we saw him floating lifelessly away, but we couldn't reach him. A twenty-foot shark would have increased our rations considerably.

D'Amour failed even more toward evening; kept asking for food and water. In his delirium he couldn't grasp our predicament. It was then that Corporal Jim Hosegood's true courage and worth began to show. Jim was a little fellow. He had to be, for he was our tail gunner—and a darn good one, too. Jim's legs were bad, probably worse than any of the rest of ours, but not according to Jim. D'Amour was Jim's best friend. They had crossed the States together on the way out to the Pacific, and now Jim began talking about the places where they had stayed—how good the beer had been at one joint, the taste of the steaks at another. He cuddled

D'Amour in his arms from then on, trying to warm him, talking to him quietly. Jim was the only one who could calm D'Amour. They spent the night that way, with only an occasional soothing word from Jim necessary to keep his friend from raving.

Sharks, real and imaginary, followed us all night —vicious fins cutting streaks in the phosphorescent water.

FOURTH DAY: As yet no boats, no islands, no airplanes. The rations became soaked during the night and were ruined, but we still kept them in hopes of drying them out. Another tiger shark attacked in the morning but was dispatched quickly. The men were all nearing collapse from exposure and lack of sleep.

We spent the morning sorting our few belongings and cleaning the automatic. We trolled all day as usual but caught no fish.

The men tried to talk cheerfully, but voices were growing hoarse and conversations rambling. Mostly they centered on home and family. The officers promised a big party if we got through O.K., and much time was spent planning this. It was going to be at Suva. Boy, that was going to be a party. We were going to drink every drop of beer on the island, and we said we'd even drink champagne if

71

we couldn't get any beer. We all talked about what we wanted most to eat. One of us just said soup and a glass of cold milk. But another would go into the minutest details in describing how his mother used to cook chicken, how thick the gravy was, the exact color of the giblets—until our dry mouths watered.

In the afternoon the raft capsized, and it took us nearly one half hour to right it. We thrashed around to scare the sharks while Jim kept D'Amour afloat even though it was a struggle. Finally we were able to right the raft and to reassemble on it. On taking inventory we found that we had half a gallon of so-called water, a few salty candy bars, and two cans of aluminum slick. The flares had been lost.

Night closed down again. By now our feet were so swollen we couldn't crowd them all into the small center of the raft. We piled them up as well as possible, crooked our arms around each other, and sat silently waiting for the sun once again.

Corporal D'Amour became much worse that night, possessed of a feverish strength. Jim held him all night again, calmly shouldering all responsibility for his friend.

Fɪꜰᴛʜ ᴅᴀʏ: Still nothing but blank horizon on all sides. The boat turned over again, but we righted it quickly. Luckily there were no sharks following us now.

Jim Hosegood was getting weak fast but wouldn't give up his duty to his friend D'Amour, who would tolerate no one but Jim. They slumped silent all day till night began to darken. We noticed then that Jim's eyes were looking glassy, and his lips white. We gave him a small sip of water and extricated D'Amour from his arms. He protested feebly at being babied, but his strength was spent.

Sergeant Rusesky and Sergeant Gagnon made a bed of their sore bruised legs across the raft and laid him on that. He talked of his many friends and planned enthusiastically the big party we were to have, but he seemed to sense that his time was up, and soon he fell into a kind of daze.

After nightfall Corporal D'Amour leaped off the raft in his delirium and disappeared in the darkness. We paddled around a long time searching and calling for him, but the only reply was the splash of waves and the singing of the wind.

We didn't tell Jim his friend had gone, but he sensed something was wrong. He lay there worrying in his semiconsciousness until nearly midnight, then suddenly said, "Good luck, fellows," and quickly passed away. Everyone wept silently for a time, then Sergeant Gagnon said, "Lieutenant Anderson, could you say a prayer for Jim?"

Could I say a prayer for Jim? Certainly I could, but to say one worthy of his devotion and friendship was hard.

"Dear Lord," I said, "You are taking Jim from us now. We know You appreciated his true worth before we did. You knew his devotion to duty, his loyalty to friends, even better than we did. Take him, now, Lord, into the high position he so much deserves. Amen."

After these words Jim was let slowly over the side. As he disappeared from sight each man said, one by one, "Good-by, Jim."

Sᴉxᴛʜ ᴅᴀʏ: Daylight again, the men all weak but still hopeful. Nothing sighted all day and all the following night. We drank the last of the water. Barely enough to wet our mouths. Everyone was slightly delirious; evidently I was the worst. That night Lieutenant Darden covered my body with his as much as possible and, I have no doubt, saved my life by his own sacrifice.

Sᴇᴠᴇɴᴛʜ ᴅᴀʏ: Another day, and I felt much better. Sergeant Anderson was slipping fast. He knew as well as we that he couldn't last another night. As it happily turned out, we had spent our last night on the open sea.

That morning we had our first break—wo caught a flying fish. We cut him up in little pieces, and he was still wriggling when he went down the hatch. We drew lots for delicacies, such as the eyes and the liver. It wasn't much nourishment, and we can still taste the darn thing, but you'd be surprised how much stronger it made us feel.

About noon we began to hear the roar of motors but could see no planes. By that time our eyes were so sunburned that it was nearly impossible to keep them open. After midday a Navy scout plane came over, close. We waved shirts and flashed signals with can tops and spread so much of the aluminum slick that we were all covered with the stuff. The pilot eventually spotted us, circled for awhile, then flew away. He soon came back and landed near us, a beautiful landing in rough water. He hollered across that help was coming, and we all sat up, shook hands, slapped each other on the back, threw things overboard and at each other, and cried for joy.

Shortly afterward a destroyer pulled up alongside and took us aboard. We all collapsed altogether. We

Of Men and War

stayed on the destroyer that night, and the next day we were transferred to a carrier. We're still on her now, eating, sleeping, and getting our strength back.

We haven't learned the pilot's name who discovered us. When we do, about all we can say is, "Thank you." It seems a small reward for seven lives, but perhaps he will understand, being a pilot too.

"BORIE'S" LAST BATTLE

In a safe, warm, weather-tight house in the nation's capital, one evening in the autumn of 1943, I heard from a handful of its protagonists the bleak tale that follows—an account of what was surely one of the strangest ship-to-ship contests in all the long history of man's fighting at sea. It is a wild story, in which two vessels seem to become animated and possessed, like breathing animals. It is also a sad story, in which two ships and many men are lost, and in which, though there is victory for one side, it turns out to be a cold, cold win.

On a black, windy night of October, 1943, the U.S.S. *Borie*, an old destroyer numbered 215, was making a speed of seventeen and a half uncomfortable knots through Atlantic seas. She had just sunk one submarine and was looking for another.

At 1:53 A.M., a kind of electric shock hit the *Borie*'s blacked-out bridge as a voice announced contact with an unidentified craft on the surface, bearing 100 degrees, just west of south.

The commanding officer of the *Borie*, Lieutenant Charles H. Hutchins, at thirty one of the youngest destroyer captains in the U.S. Navy, was standing to the right of the helmsman in the wheelhouse, and when he learned of the contact, he lowered his head and raised his arms in a characteristic gesture —like that of a man with a club in his hand about to strike an adversary—and he shouted, "Flank speed!"

As the *Borie* gained speed, she began to pitch and pound. Destroyers are wet ships, and they are wettest at high speed. The waves that night ran fifteen and twenty feet high, and by the time the *Borie* reached twenty-seven knots, black water was knocking at the highest towers of the ship. So heavy was the sea's impact that four of the portholes on the bridge—thirty feet above water level, and made of three-quarter-inch glass—were smashed, and after that, water only a few degrees above freezing began splashing into the wheelhouse through the broken ports.

In a short time the *Borie* lost surface contact with the target. Lieutenant Hutchins at once assumed that the enemy had submerged, and he ordered the sound apparatus—the device that hunts for underwater objects by means of echoing sound waves—turned on. Soundman Second Class Lerten V. Kent had only sent out a few impulses when everyone on the bridge, listening to the sound machine's slow *ping-ping*, heard a clear and solid echo. Soundman Kent waited for a second echo before he roared: "Sound contact! Bearing one nine oh."

The *Borie* moved in slowly. Soundman Kent reported every twist in the submarine's bearing. The "talkers" on the bridge—men with power telephones to guns and engine rooms—quietly told the crew what was happening. All through the ship the men were excited. They had gone through dull months. After the first eventless cruise escorting the converted merchantman carrier U.S.S. *Card*, some of the *Borie*'s crew had hung a service flag for men transferred to other ships—to indicate that those transfers had finally gone off to war.

Borie's *Last Battle*

As the old destroyer closed the range on her quarry, Chief Torpedoman Frank G. Cronin got the "ash cans" of TNT set on their racks aft. When the *Borie* had moved directly over her target, Hutchins gave the order to drop an orthodox deep pattern. Instead of the usual small number for a pattern, however, depth charges began flying off the stern one after another in an almost endless procession; something had gone wrong with the depth-charge-releasing mechanism. Soon Soundman Kent could hear the rumble of many underwater explosions in the sensitive sound stack. To mark the point of attack, Hutchins ordered a floating flare to be dropped.

The depth-charge attack forced the submarine to the surface. Hutchins thought the adversary might come up on its right and behind him, so he ordered his four-inch guns trained over the starboard quarter. But the wily German turned around under water before surfacing. This was the beginning of a series of tricks on both sides which gave this duel its weird quality.

The first man to see the U-boat on the surface was Fire Controlman First Class Robert Maher. When the submarine popped up to port and astern, Maher forgot his formal naval vocabulary and screamed, "There it is—just to the right of the flare!"

It was four hundred yards away, huge and almost white.

As if by reflex, with only a moment's thought, Lieutenant Hutchins decided that he could swing his ship around faster than the gun crew could traverse their four-inch guns to bear on the target, so he put his head down, raised his right arm in his clubbing gesture, and roared to his helmsman, Seaman Third Class James M. Aikenhead, to put the wheel hard right—away from rather than toward the submarine. Hutchins ordered the searchlight turned on. This lit up the sleek gray target, but it also gave the Germans something to aim at.

The *Borie* got the first shot in, with the Number Four gun, astern, about halfway through the circling turn. It missed. Then all the *Borie*'s guns opened fire. Men on the *Borie* could see Germans scrambling out on the conning tower to man the machine guns there.

The *Borie* straightened out and went after the submarine, verging to the right so that as she caught up she would be broadside to the enemy. The submarine could make about twelve knots, and the *Borie* was now pounding out twenty-seven again.

The gun duel was one-sided. The Germans never attempted to man their big deck gun, for the

U-boat's deck was awash, and great waves were breaking over the gun. In any case, the second or third salvo from the *Borie* lifted that gun off the deck and threw it in the sea. Sailors of the *Borie* later said they saw the gun in mid-air.

Soon the destroyer began to put up alongside the submarine, and Americans could see Germans clearly and close to. The U-boat had apparently been surprised, because several Germans were obviously straight out of their bunks; they came out on the conning tower in the nearly freezing night in nothing but underwear pants. Some were dressed in sweaters and shorts, others in dungarees. Many wore bandannas of green, yellow, and red; those without bandannas had very long hair.

When the destroyer's machine guns found the conning tower, the German guns fell silent and never fired again. As each German ran toward a machine gun he would be killed. There were times when no Germans were visible, and then, in response to long training to pick out some specific target, whether human or not, gun captains began shouting, "Bend up their guns! Get those —— guns bent up."

The U-boat commander, realizing that he was outgunned, tried to outmaneuver Lieutenant Hutchins.

He swung left and aimed his stern, which carried
the sting of torpedo tubes, at the destroyer. Hutchins
swung left, too, at first gently, hoping to stay broadside to the U-boat on the outer of two parallel
curves. But the German, circling tightly, kept his
stern aimed at the *Borie* and fired a torpedo, which
missed. At that Hutchins had Aikenhead turn full
left rudder, which made the German think the
Borie was going to cut across the U-boat's stern and
come up inside its curve. Therefore the German
straightened out. Hutchins turned hard right again
and the situation was just what it had been a few
moments before—the two ships running on roughly
parallel courses, with the destroyer a little behind
the U-boat but overtaking it.

For the next few minutes the *Borie*'s guns
drummed the submarine. The electric firing circuit
of the forecastle gun stopped working. Gun Captain
Kenneth J. Reynolds fired the gun once by pulling
the lanyard, but it broke. Rather than taking the
time to find a piece of string to make an new lanyard, he began to trip the firing pin with his hand.
He could not get his hand out of the way in time
to beat the swift recoil, so his forearm and wrist
were severely pounded and later swelled up to three
times normal size. All the time the heavy seas were

breaking over the forecastle gun, and a Negro mess attendant, Steward's Mate Second Class Ernest Gardner, twice grasped and saved a man from being washed overboard.

The *Borie* caught up with the German and began to pull ahead.

The men of the *Borie* had dreamed, as in wartime all destroyermen dream, of ramming the side of an enemy submarine and putting it down. Many times, at the wheel, Helmsman Aikenhead had talked of ramming. Just three days before, Lieutenant Hutchins had jokingly taken a piece of chalk and drawn on the center porthole, directly in front of the helmsman's eyes, three concentric rings and two lines crossing at their center. He called it the *Borie's* ramming sight. Now, therefore, Hutchins put his head down and lifted his clubbing arm and shouted, "All right, Aikenhead, line her up. Get the sight on."

Aikenhead spun the wheel and in a few seconds quietly said, "All right, sir, I got her on."

Hutchins shouted an order to be passed on to the crew: "All stations stand by for ram!"

The talkers bent their heads and said into their phones in the parroting, singsong voice of all talkers, "All stations stand by for ram."

The German seemed to be holding his course, as if unaware of his danger. It appeared that there would be a collision.

Men on the destroyer braced themselves for the shock and the pleasure. Hutchins rushed out into the open on the left wing of the bridge and held tight to the windscreen there. Aikenhead embraced the wheel. Gunnery Officer Walter H. Dietz, Jr., topside on the director platform, fell in love with the range finder and hugged it tight. Everyone was set.

Then in the last few seconds the German swerved sharply left and a huge wave lifted the *Borie*.

These two things made the moment of impact a disappointment to all hands. There was no shock. No one could hear a crunching noise. The wave lifted the *Borie*'s bow high and put it gently on the deck of the submarine, just forward of the conning tower. Momentum and the thirty-degree angle imposed by the German made the *Borie*'s bow slide forward on the submarine's. There was scarcely any damage to either craft. In the *Borie*'s forward engine room no one even knew the ships had met until the order came down to stop all engines.

And so the two ships came to rest, bow over bow, at an angle, locked in a mortal V.

Disappointment at the collision at once gave way to a crazy elation when the men on the destroyer saw how they had the German pinned down. Lieutenant Hutchins worked his clubbing arm, as if beating someone's brains out, and roared, "Fire! Fire! Open fire!" Then he just yelled, "Yipee!"—over and over. Men on the bridge threw their arms around each other and danced, shouting. "We've got the ——, we've got the ——!"

The searchlight bathed the conning tower, and all guns that could bear opened up at a thirty-foot range. For their part the Germans did not lack a mad courage. They kept coming out of the conning-tower hatch and trying to get to their guns, even in death agonies trying to man their hopeless guns. The sight was a horrible one. Some shells took Germans and pitched them bodily overboard. One German was hit squarely in the chest by a twenty-millimeter shell; his head and shoulders flew one way, his trunk another.

The situation affected different men in different ways. Range Finder Operator Seaman First Class Carl Banks, ordinarily a shy, quiet, gentle boy, finding himself now with nothing to do since range had been reduced to zero, marched up and down the director platform shouting, "Kill 'em! Kill 'em!"

Other men were elated and laughed loudly and cracked jokes. Seaman Second Class Edward N. Malaney walked to the left wing of the bridge and, amazed at the size of the submarine, said, "My God, what's that? The *Bremen*?" Other men went quietly about their work. Chief Quartermaster William Shakerly kept taking thorough notes in his log, and in the chartroom Executive Officer Lieutenant Philip Brown meticulously completed his plot of the course of action.

Then in the middle of the bedlam Brown went out on the bridge and reported to the captain. He saluted and said, "I've secured the plot, sir. To hell with charting this battle. All the essential facts are right underneath us." Brown went to the flag bags, where small arms were stowed, and picked himself out a Tommy gun. Gunnery Officer Dietz looked down on him from the director platform a few minutes later. He saw his quiet-spoken friend standing there, with his rimless glasses on, waiting coolly until a German torso lifted itself on deck across the way, then raising his Tommy gun like a professor raising a pointer at a blackboard, and pulling the trigger.

All through the ship, men acted now on their own. The phrase "people's war" came into Hutchins' mind as he watched his men. He gave very few orders. The men responded to the months of careful training that Executive Officer Brown had given them, and to their own initiative.

Everyone found something to do.

Standing on the galley deckhouse only about fifteen feet away from the conning tower, Fireman First Class David F. Southwick pulled a five-inch knife out of its sheath and threw it at a German who was running for a gun. Chief Boatswain's Mate Walter G. Kurz picked up an empty four-inch shell case weighing nearly ten pounds, waited for a German to climb out of the tower hatch, and threw the shell case at him; his target, a young boy, fell into the sea. Chief Gunner's Mate Richard W. Wenz, the strongest man on the ship, who could pick up huge depth charges alone and set them on their racks, now could not be bothered to find the key to the small-arms locker, so he broke the wooden door down with his fist. He distributed pistols, shotguns, rifles, and Tommy guns to all free hands. Seaman Malaney, unable to find any other weapon, fired a Very pistol, whose signal flares could not kill but could burn.

The gun crews worked as automatically as their weapons and with frantic urgency. Some machine guns should not have been fired, because they had steel splinter shields between them and the submarine, but the crews, at risk to their own lives, fired the guns through the shields, so as to tear them open, and the guns thereafter had fairly clear fields of fire. Loaders were injured by flying steel from the splinter shields. Officers' Cook Christopher Columbus Shepard, first loader on Number Four gun, deciding that ammunition was not coming to him fast enough, ran to the afterdeckhouse racks, grabbed a heavy shell, thrust it home, climbed into the seat of the firing pointer, who had been temporarily blinded, fired, climbed out, ran for another shell—and kept his gun going that way.

Gunnery Officer Dietz—who at the drop of a hat will quote Nelson: "No captain can do very wrong if he lays his ship alongside that of an enemy"—had trained a boarding party, and he was eager to lead it onto the submarine. But Hutchins passed this word: "We will not board. We will not board."

He had a reason for his order. The fight above-decks was going very well. Something like thirty-five Germans had been killed, and nobody had been killed on the *Borie*. But serious reports were coming up to the bridge talkers from the bowels of the ship. The engine rooms were flooding.

The German enemy had not done this to the *Borie*: the power of the sea had done it. The high waves had twisted the two ships, had reduced the V until the grappled hulls lay nearly parallel, and had pounded the shells together. The submarine, built to withstand tremendous underwater pressures, was better able to survive the grinding than the destroyer, whose skin was only three sixteenths of an inch thick. Water began pouring into both engine rooms. In the after one, a damage control party was able to stuff the leaks enough so that pumps could keep the water down, but the forward engine room became hopelessly flooded.

There the water crept up, first to the men's ankles, then to their knees. Since the engines were steamtight from within, they were, of course, watertight from without, and they kept going even when partially submerged. As the ship rolled and pitched, the water tore every mobile thing free, and soon the men were being sloshed around the engine room along with floor plates, gratings, small casks, and other dangerous debris. Machinist's Mate Second Class Ed M. Shockley and Fireman First Class Mario J. Pagnotta crawled and floated in behind some live steampipes dragging mattresses behind them, to try to plug the holes; but their efforts

washed out. Chief Engineer Lieutenant Morrison
R. Brown ordered everyone to leave. He stayed
alone to do what he could.

Finally, ten minutes after the ramming, the two
ships worked free of each other. The incredible con-
test of wit and maneuver began again.

The submarine pulled ahead and out to the left,
and Lieutenant Hutchins could see that the enemy
intended to aim his stinger at the destroyer again,
and to fire more torpedoes. That made Hutchins de-
cide to fire torpedoes of his own. He ordered the
tubes manned. Torpedo Officer Ensign Lawrence S.
Quinn made the proper calculations and fired, but
a heavy sea threw the aim off, and the torpedo
missed.

The U-boat went into a tight left circle, and the
Borie did, too. But the submarine's turning radius
was smaller than the destroyer's, and the two ships
traveled in concentric circles. Most of the time the
U-boat had its threatening tail aimed straight at the
destroyer. A four-inch hit on the submarine's starboard diesel exhaust may have penetrated to the
torpedo room and prevented the firing of any more
torpedoes.

Hutchins felt frustrated by his ship's inability to

turn on a shorter radius than the enemy. He kept having the illusion that his ship was going in a straight line, while the submarine was turning away. He did not want to lose his victim at this late hour, and he kept beating the air with his right arm and shouting over and over, "All right, Aikenhead, bring her left, dammit, bring her left."

Helmsman Aikenhead, who weighed only one hundred thirty pounds and was very tired from the stiffness of the *Borie's* wheel, kept saying in a pleading voice, "But Captain, I am left, I am left."

Hutchins would not believe Aikenhead until he looked at the compass, which was moving around fast. The captain did not know how many times the two ships made that dizzy circle. All the time he had in the back of his mind his planned rendezvous next morning with the *Card* and her other destroyers, the *Goff* and the *Barry*. He did not want to lose his position, so it was a relief, as the *Borie* turned in those merry-go-round circles, to catch glimpses of his original floating flare. The ships had made many convolutions but had not moved far.

The circling was of no advantage to the *Borie*, so Hutchins turned out his light, hoping that the U-boat would attempt to shake off the destroyer by sneaking out of the tight circle and away. The submarine tried to do just that. Hutchins snapped on the light again and soon found the glistening U-boat streaking off in a northeasterly direction. Range was four hundred yards. The *Borie* pursued.

All through the battle, so far, the *Borie* had been to the right of its adversary. Hutchins decided to break through to the other side, so while he chased the enemy he pulled left. He now gave a command that helped to win the battle: He ordered depth charges set shallow. Aikenhead was about to collapse at the wheel, so the captain ordered the helmsman relieved.

In spite of the failure of the first ramming, sinking the enemy by crashing into him was still an obsession of Hutchins and of others aboard the *Borie*. The destroyer pulled up to the left of the U-boat, and Hutchins ordered a collision course. The submarine again held its course until the last moment. This time, instead of turning sharply away as he had the first time, the German turned hard toward the *Borie*.

This brought up something entirely unexpected: The U-boat captain had decided to pull the temple pillars down and ram the destroyer. With her thin skin the *Borie* stood to lose everything by being rammed.

Hutchins had an instantaneous flash of combat inspiration. To everyone's puzzlement on the bridge, he ordered the new helmsman to turn hard left, and he ordered the starboard engine stopped, the port engine backed full. This had the effect of throwing the ship into a skidding stop, with the stern end swinging to the right toward the oncoming submarine. At precisely the correct moment Lieutenant Hutchins lowered his head and raised his nonexistent club and shouted to Depth Charge Officer Ensign Lawrence Quinn, "O.K., Larry, give 'em the starboard battery."

Ensign Quinn flicked three switches. Three round shapes arched in the wind and fell within a few feet of the submarine—two on one side and one on the other. They went off shallow. The submarine lurched out of the water like a hurt whale and came to a stop very close to the *Borie's* flank. Men on deck said that if there had been another coat of paint on either vessel, there would have been a collision.

Somehow the German submarine managed to start up again. It was like a wounded creature that refuses to die and in the very act of dying refuses to admit that it is dying. The U-boat slipped around astern of the *Borie* and drove off at an angle.

By this time the Americans, though for the most part unhurt, were dazed by the stubbornness of the enemy. The officers on the bridge were hazy about what happened next. There were various zigs and zags; apparently the *Borie* closed in to a convenient range.

Now at last the U-boat captain seemed to realize he was beaten. He sent up distress signals—white, green, and red flares. A moment later Lieutenant Hutchins saw an answering signal from the horizon. He went to the compass and checked the bearing of this other enemy—220 degrees.

The four-inch gunners gave the U-boat its final crippling blow. They hit the starboard diesel exhaust again. The submarine dropped to four knots. The *Borie* closed to point-blank range.

The Germans seemed to be trying to abandon ship. They huddled on the conning tower. With a compassion which he later did not quite understand, Hutchins ordered all guns to cease firing. But before the order reached all stations Gun Captain Kenneth Reynolds, who was still firing his gun painfully by hand, got off one last round. It blew the entire bridge structure, with all its occupants, right off the U-boat.

Water from the hole by the exhaust poured into

the submarine. Its bow lifted dripping out of the rough sea. The ship slipped under the waves and exploded with a deep rumble under water. After one hour and four minutes of tenacious fighting the submarine sank.

At once Hutchins turned his ship away.

The *Borie* was in serious trouble. Only one engine would run. Her maximum speed was now ten knots, which a surfaced submarine could easily exceed. The ship was still taking water forward. The generators were out. The water condensers were impaired, so the turbines were not getting the pure, saltless steam they needed. Hutchins reported by radio to the *Card*, "Just sank Number Two in combined depth-charge attack, gun battle, and ramming. May have to abandon ship."

Hutchins tried desperately to get the ship to the rendezvous, which was set for dawn. He gave the order to lighten ship. Everything that could be was thrown over the side: both anchors and their chains, ammunition, machine guns, torpedoes and their huge mounts, depth charges, the searchlight, range finder, fire director, and hundreds of smaller things. A hole was cut in the lifeboat and it was let over the side to sink—for it had the number 215 on it, and if left afloat it might identify the *Borie* to the enemy.

During this process Storekeeper First Class Joseph San Philip came to the bridge holding in his hand the Title B Book, which contained a list of things aboard ship for which the captain had had to sign his personal responsibility. Storekeeper Philip said, "Sir, who's going to sign out all this Title B stuff we're throwing away?"

Without saying a word Lieutenant Hutchins took the Title B Book from the storekeeper's hands and dropped it, too, into the sea.

Dawn broke overcast: The *Card*'s planes would have a hard time finding the *Borie*. The emergency gasoline generator for the radio had used up its fuel, so the destroyer was now silent.

The officers sat around the radio room, wondering what to do. Someone took out a cigarette and lit it with a lighter. Lieutenant Robert H. Lord remembered having seen some lighter fluid on another officer's desk. Word was passed through the ship to send all lighter fluid to the radio shack. The generator worked long enough on contributions from the crew for Radio Operator Cameron G. Gresh to send: "Can steam another two hours. Commencing to sink."

At 9:00 A.M. so much salt had built up in the turbines that the blades locked, and the destroyer went dead in the water.

The only hope now was that planes from the *Card* would find the *Borie*. If the *Borie* could send out radio signals the chances of their doing so would be much better. Someone thought of the alcohol in sick bay, and after it had been cut with kerosene it worked the generator all right. Radioman Gresh sent out: "Getting bad." Then he sat tapping out three dots and a dash—the letter which in all Allied lands had come to stand for Victory. A plane rode that letter in and found the *Borie*.

The *Card*, the *Barry*, and the *Goff* steamed up at about noon. The *Card* inquired by signal light how things were going. Hutchins replied, "I want to save this bucket if I can. Give me a few hours."

But things went from bad to worse. Executive Officer Brown inspected the ship. This took as much courage as the battle itself had taken. He forced himself into most of the ship's compartments, never knowing which hatch would be the last he opened. His reports indicated that it would be hopeless to try to save the ship.

Toward dusk the *Card* and her escorts returned. It was too rough for a rescue ship to go alongside the *Borie*, and there would not be time for men to be transferred by breeches buoy. There was nothing to do but have them get into the bitterly cold water and cling to rafts.

After his men were off, Hutchins went to his room and found a flashlight. And then the young captain went, alone and miserable, through the various deserted compartments of his first ship—into the fire-rooms and engine rooms, the commissary stores and messing compartments, into officers' country and the wardroom, and finally back to his own domain, the skipper's cabin. The ship was all dark and silent. All hands had abandoned her. So the captain went out on deck and, with the battle flag of U.S.S. *Borie* under his arm, slipped over the side into the frigid water.

Not a man had been lost in the fight; twenty-seven were lost in that water. For those who died it must have been much as it was for Gunnery Officer Dietz, who was nearly lost. A slender man, he had never thought himself strong. When he first hit that breath-taking water he thought it would quickly kill him, but he managed to cling to a raft until the *Goff* drifted down on it. He grabbed a life line and pulled himself up so that his hands held the edge of the deck and safety. But his hands were so cold that he could not hold on, and he fell back into the water. He slipped along the side of the ship, held up by his life belt—a mere rubber tube under his arms. Life lines caught at his throat. The *Goff*'s framelike propeller guards hit him in the head and pushed him under. He thought, "I must get away from this and wait." He pushed away from the ship. But when he tried to paddle back, his arms would hardly move. His mind refused to admit defeat and kept shielding him from fear. "They'll come after me," he kept saying to himself. He fainted. Luckily for him his head fell backward instead of forward. A few minutes later hands pulled him aboard the *Barry*.

The margin of luck was not quite so wide for those who drowned. Ensign Richard F. St. John had pulled himself halfway up a life line onto the *Goff* when he dropped back into the water to help four men who were too far gone to help themselves. They made it. Ensign St. John was caught under the destroyer and drowned. Engineering Officer Brown, who had tried bravely alone to keep the *Borie*'s engines going in water that was, near the end, up to his waist, was lost. So was Ensign Lord, who had probably saved many lives by thinking of lighter

101

fluid for the radio. The enlisted men who were lost were: Alford, Blane, Blouch, Bonfiglio, Cituk, Concha, Demaid, Duke, Fields, Francis, Kiszka, Lombardi, Long, McKervey, Medved, Mulligan, Pouzar, Purneda, Shakerly, Swan, Tull, Tyree, Wallace, Winn.

Lieutenant Hutchins could not stand up when he was taken onto the *Goff* in the darkening evening. Later he took a hot shower and shook under the steam. Then he had a rubdown, some hot chocolate, a sip of brandy, and a little exercise. He spent most that night on the bridge, waiting for dawn and a glimpse of his ship.

At sunrise the *Goff* made a last sweep for survivors. She found ten men face down in their preservers. Then she went to the *Borie*. The destroyer had drifted several miles and had settled badly.

Hutchins stood on a strange bridge and watched his ship as a Grumman Avenger attacked with a heavy bomb and missed. A second plane hit her amidships. A third holed her again, badly. The *Borie*, her back broken, lifted her protesting bow and then settled fast.

FRONT SEATS AT SEA WAR

This is the story of a Patrol Torpedo-boat squadron that fought in the Solomon Islands in the first year of combat against Japan in World War II. This was, indeed, the first American torpedo-boat squadron to have actual fighting duty—not just occasional guerrilla actions sneaking in on anchored shipping, but real brushes with warships, night after night, for months. The squadron of which Lieutenant John F. Kennedy was a member followed this one into the Solomons area.

The three boat captains who told the story to me —Lieutenant (j.g.) Leonard Nikoloric, Lieutenant Henry Stillman Taylor, and Lieutenant Robert Searles—had the humility to realize that the real heroes of PT boats, of the whole Navy for that matter, were the enlisted men.

That is why this story is told in the first person plural. There was no one hero in this squadron; no three or four men stood out above the others. The squadron was its own total hero.

We formed up in Panama.

Most of the men figured Panama was their last chance at civilization. There was a lot of time spent enthusiastically on drinking, gambling, and women. Legg, Nik's quartermaster, who was one of the finest navigators any of us had seen, would get dressed up in the evening, all in his dress whites, and he would disappear by himself. Later we would find him sitting all alone at some bar drinking beer. He was diffident, and if we offered him a drink he would be shy about accepting it. He would have six or seven beers and then go back to the base, still alone. Before retiring, while still feeling high and benign, he would tidy up his boat from top to bottom.

The men got acquainted with the boats and each other. Beed worked like a fanatic on his engines. Bracy cooked great pies. Der talked tough. Wisdom groused. Legg helped Nik on navigation. Kuharski cleaned his guns. Crosson discussed Plato and Schopenhauer, and Nale discussed the girls back home.

After the Solomons campaign began, we all figured we'd be out there sooner or later. We heard that the Marines, when they were being shelled from the sea night after night, had wondered why it couldn't be sooner rather than later.

Finally the time came. We went in two sections, four boats to a section, about ten days apart. Every PT boat comes with a cradle. They just settled the boats into their cradles and then slung boats and cradles and all right up on the deck of a cargo ship, by crane. We lived in the boats, perched up there twenty feet above the deck. It was peculiar, but it was handy for working on the bottom. We spent the whole time shining up this and that, and when we got to the South Pacific the boats were like a bunch of 4,500-h.p. Swiss watches.

During the trip Monty got pneumonia. Monty was our commanding officer—Lieutenant Commander Alan R. Montgomery, of Warrenton, Virginia. Some commanding officers are unreasonable men, but he was far from that; he was the fairest Navy man we ever knew. Most of the boat captains used to kid Monty, because he had gone to Annapolis, by referring to him as a "trade-school man," and by saying he "went to some academy—what was the name of that academy?" He would take it in stride, and he gave as good as he got, too. Monty was terribly sick on the way out.

Everything was snafu when the first section reached the rear base in the South Pacific. Apparently no one had figured in advance how they would get the boats off the ship. Those boats weighed fifty tons. When we arrived, the Seabees were at work on a huge floating crane, and still it was three weeks before the boats got into the water. No one seemed to know where we were supposed to go, where our base would be. We had to wait, and so did the Marines, for the admirals to make up their minds.

We heard about how Japs were coming down every night and shelling Guadalcanal, and we talked about how we would sink the whole Japanese fleet. The Japs were starting down from an island called Bougainville, so we used to say, "We'll derail the Bougainville express." We were pretty cocky then.

The first section's trip north to the Solomons was tough. We went in tow behind two old four-pipers converted to be Marine transports. There were two boats behind each can, and it was up to us to keep our helms over and keep clear of each other.

It took a real man to make us fast again when one of the towlines broke. On Stilly Taylor's boat, for instance, Wisdom always did it. Hobert Denzil Wisdom, Stilly's torpedoman, was a great hulk of a fellow, well-built and tough-looking, with a slight paralysis of the face which gave him a queer, ugly look. He was the squadron's champion growler; the other men always expected him to jump in first with the gripes. He grumbled like hell about fixing those

towlines, but he did the job. The towline had to be
made fast through a towing eye right at the chine,
the point at the forefoot where all the plane sur-
faces of the bow met. Wisdom had to go over the
side in water that wasn't too warm, and he had to
work down there with that huge hawser where the
bow was pitching and pounding on the seas. Stilly
had to keep the boat almost nuzzled against the port
quarter of the tow ship, so there was a chance of
Wisdom's getting crushed like a beetle between the
boat and the ship.

When he finished he was always black and blue
and grunting mad. "That's the damnedest job I ever
had to do," he'd declare, "and I won't ever do it
again." But the next time Stilly's boat broke away,
he'd be the one to volunteer to do the job.

The only joy on the trip was the food that Bracy
cooked. There was only a tiny oven about the size
of a breadbox in the galley, but he would bake
custard pies and lemon-meringue pies that made
you think of mother. Henry Duff Bracy was one of
the happiest guys that ever rode a boat, and his
everlasting bad joke was that he was itching to
make mincemeat out of some Japs.

By the time we got to Tulagi, on October 12,
Monty was thin and weak. He'd had so much sulfa

drug that he had water blisters all over his skin. The very first day he went ashore over on Guadalcanal and spent all day talking with people—getting the word. We based ourselves—and braced ourselves —in Tulagi Harbor.

We didn't have to wait long.

Our first attack came the night of October 13—the night after we arrived. We encountered more than our share of the Japanese Navy that night. There were probably three cruisers, one battleship, and about eight destroyers, which came down to give the airfield and the Marines one of their worst pastings.

PT boats ought to be manned by cats. Cats might have been able to see what was going on that night; we couldn't. All we could see was the flash of gunfire in a tight formation which was moving down from Cape Esperance to Lunga Point at about twenty knots, swinging out and around and back again—and the tracers arching ashore.

We were eager. We closed with the enemy—fast. Wisdom was standing at his battle station by an aftertorpedo tube with a mallet in his hand, ready to fire by percussion in case the electrical impulse didn't work. All of a sudden he looked up and you could hear him cursing. Stilly had taken the boat incredibly close to a Jap destroyer without even seeing it.

Being that close was bad, because there wasn't time to square away and fire a torpedo, and the Japs picked up the boats in their lights. Monty got off his torpedoes, Tom Kendall was fired on, Bobby tore over to help us, and everything was confused.

Bobby saw a target loom up. He fired—and a terrible clatter began, like that of a car running with a burnt-out bearing. One torpedo had shot away all right, but two of the torpedoes had stuck halfway out of their tubes and were having hot runs. Torpedoes have to run a certain distance through the water before a little mechanism up in the warhead "arms" them so they will explode. Ordinarily in hot runs the fish don't get armed, but if the boat is running fast—as Bobby's soon had to run—spray can get up in there and arm them, so that after that a seven-pound blow can kiss the boys good-by.

When Beed, Bobby's elderly engineer, heard all the clatter, he thought the boat was under machine-gun fire. He clamped all the engine-room hatches shut so as to make the engine room light-tight, whipped out his flashlight, and began checking his engines as calmly as if they were still in Panama.

He soon had them singing and the boat made its getaway out of the searchlight beams. Fortunately the fish did not become armed.

Soon the Japs lit out and chased our boats. The poop about PT boats making fifty knots was strictly Hudson River stuff. Under battle conditions we seldom got them going that fast. And the Jap destroyers could sometimes keep up with us. Monty, who as CO was riding in a boat with Bobby's brother Jack Searles, had a nightmare of a time. He was chased all over hell-and-gone. Finally he crept inshore and Jack cut his engines and they lay doggo. First thing they knew, the waves were driving them ashore. They were finally beached and helpless. Luckily the Japs didn't get them in their lights again.

Well, that was our first night of it. So far as we knew, we had got zero Jap ships plus one helluva scare.

About a week later Robbie, the second-in-command, came up from the rear base. Then Monty practically collapsed and had to be evacuated; it broke his heart to have to leave. Although only a twenty-seven-year-old lieutenant, Hugh Marston Robinson took over the squadron and from then on did all the administrative work and tactical planning.

The tension of running patrols night after night, working all day, not knowing what was coming next, was severe at first. Robert Charles Barnard, a machinist's mate on Stilly's boat, was so nervous on some of the first patrols that he had to go out on deck and turn handsprings and somersaults. After a while, though, we began to be able to relax a little and think about our comforts. For instance, Nik's shoes wore out, and he found time one day to go over to Tulagi to get some new ones. He came on a Marine who'd been evacuated from the Guadalcanal beachhead with malaria. Nik asked him where he could get a pair of those nice soft Marine shoes.

"You want some lucky shoes?" the Marine asked.

"Sure do," Nik said.

"I've got some for you. They ain't new. They're lucky though. You better take 'em. They belonged to a pal of mine—he got killed. He went out on patrol after patrol and he killed a slew of Japs—as long as he wore these here shoes. But one day he went out in another pair. He came on a Jap dugout, and he jumped in and pulled the trigger of his Reising gun, but it just went click. He should've worn his old shoes. You want 'em?"

Nik took them and wore them every time he went out.

Nik was glad to have his lucky shoes on October 28. That was when the second section had its first serious action.

Some of the first section happened to be out that night, too. The two brothers, Bobby and Jack Searles, were riding a boat together, doing some spotting. Stilly had the same assignment. Brent Green was up the line in Jap territory trying to "lead" a reported force of eight or ten Jap destroyers in to us—in other words, he was tracking them, so we could attack them at an opportune place and time.

We of the second section were fat, dumb, and happy that night. We couldn't wait to bore in there and make an attack and get baptized. All the men were in high. John Der, a tough and audible character from Akron, Ohio, who had the most patriotic eagle tattooed all the way from his shoulders to his belly button, kept running up to Nik's bridge and saying, "We'll sink 'em. We'll sink 'em all. Don't worry, Skipper, we'll sink 'em."

The Japs came in under the front of a big black cloud. We couldn't see them. There were flares and shots fired toward the beach, but every time we ran toward them there wouldn't be anything there.

The Searles's radioman, Stevenson, suddenly came up on the radio and said, "We're being chased by William. Hurry, hurry, hurry." At that time "William" meant enemy ships.

Nik decided to run in and take the heat off the Searles brothers. Legg said, "Skipper, you can't go home and face Mrs. Searles if both those boys get it tonight." Nik opened up wide and plunged into the smoke screen Bobby and Jack had left; the boys on his boat expected to see the whole Jap Navy on the other side of the screen.

They saw nothing. The destroyer had apparently got word that a whole swarm of PT boats was after it and had turned to run. By great good luck it turned so as to make a perfect shot for Brent Green. He fired a spread and the Jap was sunk. . . .

That was how the battles went. The boys who thought they were going to be heroes didn't turn out to be. Someone would just be surprised into a success.

By this time we were beginning to get our base established. The men hewed out a nook of civilization ashore. Our base was on an island we called Cannibal Isle. The men would find themselves a place to pitch a tent and go to work.

The only way Wisdom could keep himself from grousing was to be doing something with his hands, so he set up a tent, built a deck for it, and made himself some fancy furniture. Others followed his lead. Some pitched their camp around the bay, others in a settlement on a bluff which they named Snob Hill—three native huts and some tents. The fellows up there kept their place as clean as a town. They had little ditches for drains. They built a bench out in front of their tents which they called the Seat of Meditation. They maintained their own iron discipline; strong-armed Wisdom was the justice of the peace.

On off nights the men would sit together in a tent, four or five of them together, and play blackjack or checkers or red dog or poker. Mostly poker. But the main amusement was shooting the breeze. Crosson would discuss various historical facts with anyone who would listen, but sooner or later, of course, the discussion always got around to girls.

Sometimes the men would compare tattoos. Der would explain the fine points of the huge eagle on his chest, and Leon Nale would demonstrate the multicolored lion's head on his shoulder and show

115

how shaggy it was, as well as the scene of crossing the equator, and the girl, very suggestive, on his forearm.

This Nale was only nineteen, one of the youngest boys in the squadron, but he was as tough as the thing his name sounded like. He was fresh; called his skipper not "sir" but "Rumdum." "Say, Rumdum, you sure hacked that one," he would say after a patrol. For a while he gave us plenty of laughs by trying to raise a mustache. He was so young that it was three weeks before we could even see the peach down except in a strong light. "Ain't that wonderful, just like Clark Gable," he would say, cocking his face up. The others finally put him down one day and shaved the fuzz off.

The days ashore grew more and more pleasant; the nights at sea grew less and less so. We called November our Hell Month. It really was.

Early in November the Japanese were making landings on Guadalcanal at Koli Point, to the east of the Marines' beachhead. This was the first time they had tried to land to the east since August, and it was important for us to interfere with their landings. A typical night was that of November 4.

We were patrolling off Koli Point. In Nik's boat

Legg had the glasses. Nik could not see a sign of the enemy. Finally Legg, instead of shouting that he had sighted the Japs, quietly said, "Sir, how many of us did you say were out tonight?"

Nik said, "Two boats, besides us," knowing very well that Legg knew how many there were.

Legg said, "Mmm. I count one, two, three, four. . . . Well, sir, I guess this is it."

So Nik practically split his throat yelling, "General quarters!" The men rushed to their battle stations.

The boat turned toward the nearest ship, to get in a good lick. Legg conned Nik in, calling off the enemy's course and speed. Some of the crew yelled from their battle stations, "What is it?"

Nik yelled back, "I think it's a destroyer."

They were moving full throttle now, with a good roar. Legg kept saying, politely and quietly, "I suggest you come right a little, sir, now come left a hair."

Suddenly Nik saw the destroyer. "Don't you think I ought to go a little closer?" he asked Legg.

Legg said, "Excuse me, sir, I think you're close enough, Skipper. If you want to shoot, shoot now."

Crosson had the tubes all set, fanned out at an angle. (Torpedoes have a gyroscopic mechanism that allows them to be shot at an angle, then turns them onto their proper course.) Nik pressed the impulse buttons. The boat shied like a skittish horse. A spread of four fish hissed into the water. All four ran their courses and missed. Pearle, Nik's radioman, said on the radio, "We missed. The enemy is moving south."

Robbie, the commander, could not find the destroyer. He came up on the radio and said, "Where the hell is he? I don't see anything. What are you guys doing, anyway?"

The next thing we all heard was Cavanaugh, Les Gamble's radioman. He was practically singing, "We got a hit! We got a hit! We're heading for the barn. We got a hit. . . ."

The enlisted men knew the practical things. They were technicians. The officers were selected for qualities of leadership and were trained in tactical command under wartime conditions. They didn't have the time to learn the details, but they could give their men confidence and courage. The smartest thing they could do was to rely on their experienced enlisted men. Finally the men became self-reliant, as was proved on the night of November 8.

Nik's section was out after the Tokyo Express.

(This was the same as the Bougainville Express, only Admiral Halsey called it the Tokyo Express, and who were we to argue with him?) Nik had no idea of the Jap disposition. He bulled right in because he was determined to be "a lousy hero." The Japs found him before he found them. They turned two lights on. They straddled the boat with two salvos. The second was so close that everyone on the boat was knocked down—and out, in the case of the two officers. Before Nik came to, this is what happened:

John Der, the crewman with the eagle tattooed on his chest, got up in a daze off the deck. It ran through his spinning mind that there had been a big noise. Noise meant torpedo. He looked at his. It was still in the tube. Wham! He hit the percussion cap with his mallet. The torpedo made its run and hit a Jap!

The boat, meanwhile, was racing in the direction of the enemy, becoming a better target every second. Legg stood up, stepped over Nik's body, took the wheel, and turned the boat around.

Leon Nale, the cocky nineteen-year-old, had been in the aftercockpit manning the machine gun. He was knocked off his stance over the fuel tanks and right down into the tank compartment. He came to, scrambled up again, wheeled his gun around, and

119

knocked out both searchlights while the PT was in a fast turn.

Crosson came to, manned the smoke valves, heaved them open, and established a first-rate smoke screen.

Porterfield and Carner teased the engines so the boat made its best speed.

Pearle, the radioman, had done his job, so he dived into an empty torpedo tube.

Then Nik came to. While he had been listening to the birdies singing, his half-dazed men had executed a successful attack, broken off, and conducted a retreat.

Yes, we were busy those nights. The men were losing a lot of weight. Yet no one slacked off. Take Bracy. Most of the cooks were moved ashore into the base force, but Bracy refused to leave the boat roster. He would cook pies and cakes all day, and we would eat the stuff out on patrol, while Bracy stood lookout. He had wonderful eyes and was always spotting something. The men said he could see through a keyhole at twenty feet.

The great sea battle of Guadalcanal, November 12 to 15, was the turning point of the war in the South

Pacific. We fought part of it, and we watched part of it.

The squadron had been in action almost continuously for ten days, and we knew the Japs were making their big attempt to reinforce their beachhead on the island. Everybody was tired and had the shakes, both officers and men. On the night of the thirteenth, there were only five boats left in condition to patrol, and one patrol had already been out, so that left only three boats running. But a big Japanese battleship had been reported hanging around all day with a flock of destroyers, so we took our three rigs out against it.

First we had to screen one of our crippled ships that was being towed in. Then they sent us over for the big game. The Japs were lying over there shelling Henderson Field. They had put a flare up over the Marines, which lit things up nicely for us. One ship appeared heavier than the others; it looked like either a battleship or a heavy cruiser. Stilly got on a collision course, approached to twelve hundred yards, fired a spread, and moved away without ever having been seen. At least one torpedo found its target. Then Jack fired and got two hits on one of the screening destroyers. Our best results came from what seemed to be the easiest attacks, like this one.

We fired eighteen torpedoes that night. Every time we fired a spread, we used to think, "Golly, there go forty thousand bucks." This night we spent one hundred eighty thousand dollars. But we figured we cost the Japs much more than that.

When we came back in, there wasn't a fish left in any one of the tubes. Assembling and mounting torpedoes is a mean job. The way that task was handled the next day, so that three boats could go out with fish in them by night, was certainly a triumph for the base force.

The soul of the base force was embodied in a chief torpedoman named Long, whom we called Shorty. Shorty was a small, quiet, self-effacing man who had been in the Navy for more than twenty years. In no time at all, Shorty Long and his sidekick, another chief named Wing, had organized a respectable torpedo shop. Shorty would visit machine shops on various ships, and he would come out with his clothes bulging with tools, rope, and gizmos—then he'd say he just couldn't think how those things had got in his pockets. Malaria and dengue fever knocked Shorty out badly for a while, and he looked sixty-five when we came out, though he couldn't have been more than forty-five.

Long and Wing went to work before the sky turned from black to gray on the morning of the 14th, and they didn't knock off until it was too dark to see a thing; three boats were ready.

No torpedoes were fired that night, but for those who were out it was the most terrific night of the whole campaign.

At the port director's office that evening we were told that a Jap invasion fleet—not just a task force; this time it was an *invasion fleet*—was on its way. The Japs had destroyers, cruisers, at least one battleship, possibly two, and a whole bunch of transports.

The briefing officer also said, "We may have a battleship task force, Admiral Lee's outfit, coming up to meet the Japs, but we're not sure. Even if they do come, we don't think they'll get here in time. We want you fellows to sift through the destroyers and cruisers and get the transports."

It sounded like certain suicide. Nik, for one, was dripping with sweat when he left that office. He had never been so scared. He didn't expect to live through the night.

When Nik went aboard his boat, the crew clustered around and asked for the dope. He didn't have the heart to tell them. He said, "I don't know for sure, I think some Japs are supposed to be coming down. I'm not sure, maybe we'll get the word on the radio later."

We started out on patrol and ran up and down like frightened terriers. Finally Robbie picked up the Japs. His radioman came up with a dull voice and said, "Here they are."

Robbie came on himself, just as dull, with, "Well, let's see what we can do."

We turned, and there, just west of Savo Island, we saw them. Counting the mirages our frightened minds conjured, there were a thousand ships spread out before us. It was the greatest show of force any of us had ever imagined, much less seen. Even our boats seemed to tremble as we deployed for what we knew would be our last runs.

Just then a cheery, lilting voice, not one of ours, came up on the radio. It said, "Boys, this is Ching Chong China Lee. Do you know who I am?" We all knew that it was Admiral Lee, who had spent several years on the China station.

Robbie's deep voice boomed out on the radio, "Yes, *sir*, we sure do!"

The Admiral came back, "Get the hell out of the way. I'm coming through."

You have never seen three PT boats move the way ours did. We almost took on some altitude.

We withdrew northward, and as we did, we saw Lee go by with his force. It seemed small to us, compared with what we had seen of the Japs, but it looked like mama to us little babies.

We stopped our engines. Porterfield went below and made some sandwiches and coffee. We all went up and sat on the foredeck, and half an hour later we were all sitting there eating tunafish sandwiches, sipping coffee, and watching from a front-row seat one of the great battles of World War II. It was just like sitting at the Polo Grounds. Only different.

We sat there for a time and nothing happened. Then somebody dropped a number of flares. We don't know which side. The destroyers opened fire first with some small stuff, over near Savo Island. Ships exploded. Each explosion gave off some daylight. First we'd see a ship explode, then there'd be a huge burning for a minute or so; then there would be another explosion, then there would be the burning again.

Then the battleships began.

There would be a little flash. Three red balls

would then go into the sky, up, and over, and down, and then whoomp! A ship would blow up. It was unbelievable.

The two groups of ships were operating about five miles apart. We just sat there and watched the tracers cross the sky, and the explosions, and the fires. Those three red balls would go up and seem to hang there in the sky, and they seemed to go very slowly; then they would fall.

This went on for an hour, or maybe two or three. We just sat there on deck the whole time. We were so impressed and amazed at the sight that nobody spoke for many minutes after the thing died down. Finally one of the men said, "My God, what a sight, what a sight."

It was the terrible power of the thing that got us. You could guess what was happening there in the ships, the human lives destroyed, the men being hurt, the groans, the sunk ships, the survivors and the flotsam in the water.

As we talked it over, we spoke unnaturally, stiffly. We couldn't help it. One man said, "What a terrible loss of equipment and men we have witnessed in an hour."

When it was surely over, we sat around awhile in the dark night and talked about the damage big ships could do, and then we went home to our base.

After that night, things tapered off a bit. The Japanese had suffered a great reverse. Toward the end of the month we occasionally had a job nobody liked. That was to stay out after dawn and strafe stores that the Japs would float off destroyers on oil drums. We had become a bit feline by now; we liked nights best. Dawn made us uneasy. Men like Nale and Wisdom would say, "I don't think we ought to stay for the weekend, Skipper," or, "Hell, Skipper, I'm so hungry, let's go home before I start eating rags."

A little later on our effectiveness fell off a hundred per cent. We had had enough; we were no good any more. All of us had had malaria or dengue fever or dysentery. We had all lost ten to thirty pounds and were terribly nervous. We weren't closing properly with the enemy any more. Every time we reported in before a patrol we would be wringing with sweat. We prayed that the Japs wouldn't come down. We were no good any more. About the only thing that held us together was Robbie Robinson's leadership and understanding.

We had been incredibly lucky on casualties. We had lost only one officer and one man, and they got

127

theirs while riding in another squadron's boat. But we began to lose men to disease. Nemeck died. Silent Joe, we called him. Bobby remembered a phrase from one of his letters to his mother that he had read as censor: "It's exciting here, and naturally I'm scared. But I guess the Japs are scared, too." Peritonitis got him, not Japs.

After three months, even Wisdom wore out. Stilly had to relieve him. After his relief Wisdom suddenly looked ten years younger and nobody could get him to gripe about a thing.

We began to have disciplinary trouble. One of our gunners was a bloodthirsty kid who had had two ships sunk out from under him: the *California* at Pearl Harbor, and later the *Seminola*. He would ride on Higgins boats, carrying supplies out to the ships, a dangerous mission, just for the fun. He even fought with the Marines at the Matanikau River, to see what it was like. He lived on Snob Hill and one night some fellows needled him. They threw his bunk over a cliff. He got sore. He went down and picked himself out a couple of Tommy guns and Springfields and announced he was going to hold that hill against all comers. He was crazy mad. Everyone took to foxholes. Finally Charley Tufts went up and talked the guns away from him.

Christmas Eve was one of the unhappiest nights in all our lives. A couple of fellows were out on patrol. Robbie and Nik were standing by. Suddenly Tom Kendall, one of the boys who was out, came up on the radio, "We have sighted a Jap destroyer. We're attacking. Please send a plane from Henderson Field to check."

Robbie looked at his charts and said, "Nik, I'll bet a thousand bucks they're attacking this little island." And he pointed to an island which we, and the fliers, too, had often mistaken for a destroyer. Nevertheless, air support had been requested, and our other boats also started out.

Well, they had attacked the island. Then they started home. About that time the planes came out, spotted two PT's, thought they were Japs, and began to strafe. We all screamed on the radio, but those fliers never got the word. They just attacked and attacked. Finally the boats had to fire on them to keep them off.

Just as the fight ended, it was eight bells—midnight, and the beginning of Christmas Day. One of the boat captains said bitterly on the radio, "Boy, what a nice Christmas present *we* got."

Of Men and War

But Christmas itself was wonderful. The Navy arranged to have a real turkey dinner sent to us with all the fixings, even cranberry sauce. And they brought up wads of mail; no fighting man could ask for any nicer present than mail from home.

New Year's Eve was pretty good fun, too. We brewed some cocktails out of medical alcohol and powdered pineapple juice. We called them Tulagi Torpedoes. They were terrible, but we got nice and high.

We had a few drinks, now and again, on a New Zealand corvette that worked out of Tulagi. Its skipper was a man named Brittson who weighed two hundred and eighty-five pounds and had a laugh in every pound. He used to play the accordion, and in his wardroom he had a gadget he called the American Horse-Dung Grinder, and he would turn the handle whenever our stories got too tall.

One night Les Gamble, who was easily our highest scorer—two destroyers and several other hits—was on patrol. Communications and our dispositions were all fouled up that night. Les fired a couple of fish at what he thought was a Jap. Fortunately he missed. Brittson came up on the radio, "Are you little nitwits firing at me?"

Les had to admit weakly that he had been.

Brittson said in a lordly tone, "The bar of His Majesty's ship *Censored* will be closed to Americans for the duration."

Our particular "duration" wasn't to be much longer, thank goodness. One morning in the middle of February a mail boat came in, and someone handed a slip of paper to Nik, who happened to be on the deck. "This is it, this is it!" he screamed. He showed it to Robbie, who jumped up and down and shouted.

"It" was supposed to be a confidential document, but within sixty seconds the whole island had the news. "It's come! It's come!" Men hugged each other and cried.

The order instructed the officers and operative personnel of our squadron to proceed to another base. We were relieved at last, after four long months.

We left our boats behind. We care now but we didn't then. We were bitter then, and we thought PT's weren't good for much except to carry generals out of places. All in all, we had encountered some two hundred and fifty targets. We had only been able to claim one cruiser (Bobby and Jack Searles), six destroyers (Brent Green, Stilly Taylor, Jack

Searles, Nik Nikoloric, and two for Les Gamble),
one positive patrol ship (Jack Searles), and one
probable (Tom Kendall and Nik Nikoloric). We
had twenty-two hits altogether, and we think Les
Gamble sank two or three other ships, and Robbie,
two. But we thought that wasn't a very devastating
average. We knew we hadn't prevented the Japs
from fulfilling a single mission.

Later, when we cooled off, we knew that we had
been useful as a harassing force, and that we had
not been intended to sink the whole Jap Navy.

But bitter as we were when we left, we were at
least friends. For the boat captains, at any rate, that
was worth all the horrible things. We boat captains
mostly had gone to Ivy League colleges; we had led
rather sheltered lives. To discover what the men in
our boats were like was the best thing that could
have happened to us. We valued their loyalty and
friendship. Stilly said that the thing that pleased
him most out there was not sinking a destroyer, not
getting his Silver Star. It was having one of his men
come up one day and say, "Skipper, don't mind if
I say this, but I hope to —— we'll have a chance
to go out on a binge together some day."

They have.